INVITATION TO READ

INVITATION TO READ

An introduction to daily Bible reading
(selected readings from *Words for Today 1994, 1995 and 1996*)

IBRA
INTERNATIONAL BIBLE READING ASSOCIATION

Cover:
Woodcut by Boy Dominguez, the Philippines
(Permission sought)

Published by:
The International Bible Reading Association
1020 Bristol Road
Selly Oak
Birmingham
Great Britain
B29 6LB

ISBN 0-7197-0889-3

© 1996 International Bible Reading Association

All rights reserved. No part of this publication may be reproduced, stored in a retrieval system, or transmitted, in any form or by any means, electronic, mechanical, photocopying, recording or otherwise, without the prior permission of the International Bible Reading Association.

*Typeset by Avonset, Midsomer Norton, Bath, Avon
Printed and bound in Great Britain by
BPC Paperbacks Ltd, Aylesbury, Bucks*

CONTENTS

	Writers	Page
Introduction		7
Prayers for morning and evening		8
A surprising Saviour	Pauline Webb	13
A living community	Joseph G Donders	21
Bread of Life	Alec Gilmore	31
The Way of Suffering	Sheila Cassidy	43
Christ's Victory	M Gnanavaram	61
Psalms of Praise	Jonathan Magonet	67
Be prepared for opposition	Magali Cunha	73
The Spirit shares our struggle	Jane Montenegro	79
Responding to blindness	Jane Wallman	85
People of God	Bernard Thorogood	91
Pray for the peace of Jerusalem	Harry Hagopian	101
Peace with justice	Albert Friedlander	109
Order Form		120

Introducing IBRA

This book is intended to help those who would like to begin making a habit of regular or daily bible reading and who would like to sample IBRA's varied approach to Bible Study. It offers a selection of readings from three editions of *Words for Today* (1994, 1995 and 1996) – a taste of the compelling and challenging insights that come from our pages. The themes and readings are not related to specific dates in the calendar (our usual custom) so that you can use them at any time in the year and at your own pace.

What is special about IBRA?

IBRA is international and ecumenical. Writers of many nationalities and religious traditions, and from different professional and cultural backgrounds, bring fresh insights and distinctive approaches to Bible study. Here is an opportunity to learn from one another and to be aware of the wider fellowship within which our daily life of prayer, meditation and study is set. Since IBRA was formed in 1882, notes like these have been used in over 80 countries and some are translated into other languages. Themes relate to the Churches' Lectionary, and readers are helped to make a more systematic study of some books of the Bible.

How to use this book

* **Read the Bible passage** for the day and then the notes. Read the verses again, allowing the words to penetrate your whole being. Try to discover their message for you and the world around you. God's Word is alive and relevant, even if it does not always offer the comfort you expect. If necessary, refer back to other readings in the series, so that you see the links.

* **Don't shut out the world.** Hold the news of each day in your mind as you read the Bible and pray. Imagine yourself as a person living in an area of the world that you are concerned about, and ask yourself, 'What is God saying through these words in this situation?'.

* **Use the prayer for each day** as a 'starter' for your own prayer and meditation.

* **Action!** Our prayerful reading of the Bible should change our attitudes, so that we respond to the world around us in new ways. You will not have time to put every suggestion into practice, but do consider each one carefully so that, by the time you reach the end of this book, you will have made some new ventures in faith.

* **Keep an open mind.** If, as you read these notes, you encounter a new insight, a new challenge, or even an interpretation with which at first sight you disagree, pause and reflect: what is this saying to me? how shall I respond? Sometimes, the idea may be so new that the answers will not immediately be apparent. Do not bury the questions. Carry them in your mind and allow the Holy Spirit to lead you gradually to discover the truth.

What next?

If you have found these readings helpful and would like to continue reading the Bible the IBRA way, then please ask us to send you a copy of the current year's edition of *Words for Today*, using the order form on page 108.

If, on the other hand, you have found these notes difficult, you may like to try IBRA's other publication of daily Bible reading notes — *Light for our Path* — which has a simpler presentation, is less provocative and aims to help those who are young in faith.

We look forward to hearing from you, and hope you will accept this challenge to learn from Jewish Rabbis and Christians of many cultutres as you read the Bible. And may you grow in faith as the Holy Spirit leads you to make fresh discoveries through the insights of others.

Maureen Edwards

Maureen Edwards- Editor

MORNING PRAYERS

Father-Creator, Provider-from of-old, Ancient-of-days – fresh-born from the womb of night are we. In the first dawning of the new day draw we nigh unto Thee. Forlorn are the eyes till they have seen the Chief.

Bushman's prayer, South Africa
From Another Day, edit. John Carden (SPCK)

Jesus, is this what you say to us today?
How blest are those who abhor easy pieties;
   the kingdom of heaven is theirs.
How blest are those who train in non-violence;
   they shall have the earth for their possession.
How blest are those who fast for justice;
   they shall be satisfied.
How blest are those who see enemies as human;
   mercy shall be shown to them.
How blest are those who live what they profess;
   they shall see God.
How blest are those who build bridges of reconciliation;
   God shall call them his friends.
How blest are those who show the outcast
   that someone understands;
   the kingdom of heaven is theirs.

Peter Matheson, Aotearoa New Zealand
From Your Will be Done (Christian Conference of Asia)

Creator God, you are light:
there is no darkness in you.
Before the heat and strife of day,
in the stillness,
we rise to meditate and pray.
Gently lead us out of darkness,
bitterness and despair
into the dawn of enlightenment and reconciliation.

Maureen Edwards - written in Sri Lanka, 1988

EVENING PRAYERS

Lord, I thank Thee for night,
the time of cool and quiet,
the time of sweet enchantment
when a deep mystery pervades everything.
The time when soul speaks to soul in common desire
to partake of the hush of the ineffable.
The time when the moon and stars
speak to us of our high calling and destiny.
The time of repose and calm
when the fever of the mind subsides
and uncertainty gives place
to the sense of eternal purpose.
O Lord, I thank Thee for night.

Chandran Devenesan, India
From Another Day (SPCK)

As the earth keeps turning, hurtling through space, and
　　night falls and day breaks from land to land,
Let us remember people – waking, sleeping, being born, and
　　dying – one world, one humanity ...

From Jesus Christ, the Life of the World. A Worship Book 1983.
WCC Publications, World Council of Churches,
Geneva, Switzerland

A blessing

May wisdom herself take root in you,
grow strong and tall within you;
May she touch what is old and dead
and make you beautiful and fragrant
like cedars and olive-trees;
May she spread out her branches and shelter you;
And as the tree of life sustains and heals you,
so may your fruits and leaves be a source of life
for the world.

Alison Geary, United Kingdom
From Oceans of Prayer (NCEC)

The cross on the facing page was painted by Fernando Llort, in memory of Maria Cristina Gomez of El Salvador, a primary school teacher and member of the Baptist Church. She was brutally murdered in 1989 because she met with others in her parish to read the Bible and discuss the meaning of her faith in the context of injustice and violence. At least 70,000 others in her country were killed between 1980 and 1991 because they had the courage to make a stand for justice. The stories of their suffering must be among the bitterest of world history. The picture of this cross depicts the daily life of women, bereft by war and conflict, carrying on the responsibilities of family and community life. It remains as a symbol of hope for the Church and the world at the end of the twentieth century.

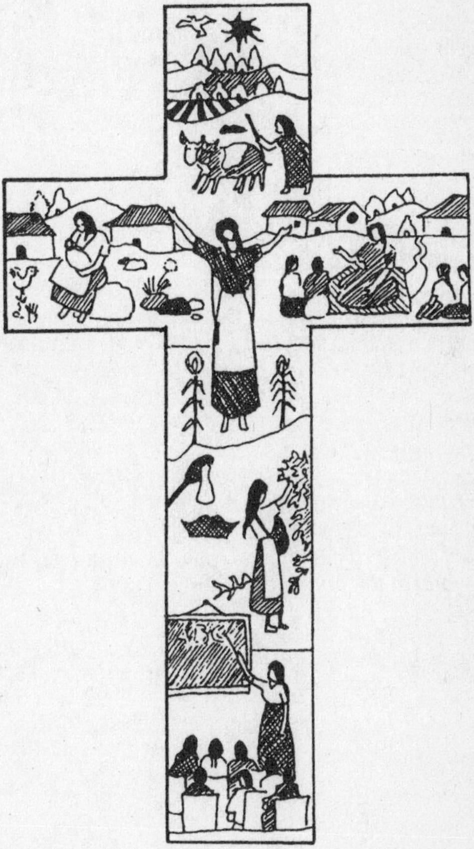

A SURPRISING SAVIOUR

Notes based on the Revised English Bible by

Pauline Webb

*People meeting Pauline Webb for the first time often comment, 'It's a surprise to meet the face behind the voice!' She is best known as a frequent broadcaster on BBC's **Thought for the Day** and **Pause for Thought** and was, for eight years, Head of Religious Broadcasting for BBC World Service. She has travelled widely, as an officer of the Methodist Church Overseas Division and as a Vice-Moderator of the World Council of Churches.*

A friend of mine who had been an agnostic for many years, eventually, towards the end of her life, became a Christian. When I asked her what finally convinced her, she replied, 'Life has been so full of surprises that I've come to believe there must be a God who keeps things up his or her sleeve. So I think of God as being like a person who loves me and never ceases to amaze me the more I get to know him.'

There's a book called *God of Surprises*, written by a Jesuit priest, Gerard Hughes (published by Darton Longman and Todd 1985). It would make excellent background reading to our theme, particularly chapters 10 and 11. The author uses three guidelines we could apply to our reading about Jesus:

- remember that he is human, like us;
- reflect that we are meant to be like him;
- realize that deep within us we can have the same spiritual resources as were available to him.

If we follow these guidelines as we read the following passages, we may be in for some surprises!

✴ ***Surprising God,***
disturb our minds
with new thoughts of you,
direct our feet
into new paths of faith,
and delight our hearts
with new hopes of heaven.
Through Jesus Christ our Lord.

Day 1   *Luke 2.41-52*

A surprising teenager

Gerard Hughes points out in his book *God of Surprises* that Luke 2.49 is the only recorded saying of Jesus from the first thirty years of his life. What does that say to us about Jesus himself as both listener and teacher? What warning does it carry for us about our anxieties for others and our inability sometimes to realize how important it is for them to make their own discoveries of faith? And what does it show us about the resources available to us as we embark on our own exploration of the Scriptures?

Teenage boys today, as in Jesus' time, are expected, at a special Bar Mitzvah ceremony, to become 'sons of the Law', able both to read from and to expound the Torah to their elders. Sometimes modern young people surprise their elders by the unsuspected depth of their understanding and maturity, if this is not stifled by over-protective parents. It has been said that 'a boy becomes a man when a man is needed'. We should never underestimate what God is doing in the life of others, especially of teenagers.

✷ *Open our eyes, O Lord,*
that we may see new truths in familiar words.
Help us to perceive how your promises
are being fulfilled
in our lives and the lives of others.

Day 2   *John 2.13-22*

Storm in the Temple!

How different is this second visit of Jesus to the Temple from his first! Then, as a young boy, he astounded the scribes by his scholarship. This time, a grown man, he alarms the money-changers by his anger. It is an anger expressed physically as well as verbally. Animals are driven out, tables overturned and people rebuked. What was it that made him most angry? – the exploitation of the poor, the greed of the money-changers, or the desecration of God's house? Perhaps, to Jesus, all these three factors together added up to blasphemy.

'Do not turn my Father's house into a market.' The young boy Jesus had delighted to be in his Father's house, doing his Father's business. So it comes as a shock to him to see that house turned into a market.

There is a sense in which today we see the whole world being turned into a market. The 'market economy' with all its dealing in currencies and its fluctuations in values affects us all and is destroying the lives of millions of our fellow men and women. How angry do we become about it? What can we do to reclaim God's world-house for all God's people?

✳ *Lord, come into the temple of my heart this day,*
and cleanse from it all that desecrates
this dwelling-place of God.
Make me as angry as you are over my sins
and the sins of our society.
Make me as ready as you are
both to condemn and to forgive them.

Day 3   Matthew 23.23-28

Blunt speaking

This chapter is the last in Matthew's Gospel that records Jesus speaking out publicly, to the whole multitude. It is probably a collection of sayings, arranged, as Matthew so often does, in one continuous discourse. It is not a condemnation of all Pharisees. Many of them were good and upright people, whom Jesus counted among his friends. But it was those who misused religion who angered him so much, particularly when they excused unjust actions and unfair attitudes with pious platitudes. People might be scrupulous about small details of religious observance, giving to the Temple a tenth of all their produce, even to the smallest herbs. But if they were unscrupulous in their treatment of others, Jesus condemned them in no uncertain terms.

Notice in verse 23 what Jesus regards as 'the weightier matters of law'. He refers to Micah 6.8 as the standard for true religious life. Which sins do religious people tend to condemn most readily today? How much prominence do we give to justice, humility and reverence as the most important moral values? How often do we speak out against hypocrisy, greed and self-indulgence?

✳ *Lord, grant that we may speak plainly*
and act honestly.
Help us to reflect our worship of you
in the respect and justice we show to all people.

Day 4 *Mark 1.9-11*

Identifying with ordinary people

Take time today to picture the scene on the bank of the River Jordan. A fiery wayside preacher has gathered around him a motley crowd of people: some hanging on his every word, others ridiculing this wild man from the desert. Then through the crowd comes the solitary figure of Jesus. John had already spoken of him in awe, as One far more worthy of honour than he is himself. Yet Jesus comes, wanting to be treated as one of the crowd, going down into the waters of baptism with the others, identifying himself with their sins.

I was once in Ethiopia at the time of the Festival of Timkat. It was the custom in those days that on the Feast of the Epiphany, the Emperor would go out into the streets, there to be publicly re-baptised, as a sign of his humility before God and the people. Then all the people too would be sprayed with the water of baptism, so that they might share in this annual cleansing.

We are not told whether anyone but Jesus saw the sign of God's favour resting upon him. We do know that he did not boast of it, but took himself away quietly to ponder all that it would mean for the rest of his ministry.

✶ *Lord, make me realize that I am one of the many*
  needing your forgiveness,
  but help me to recognize too
  that you have a special purpose for each one of us.

Day 5 *Mark 1.16-20; John 1.43-51*

Ordinary people

Why on earth do you think that, for his first disciples, Jesus chose a group of fishermen? What particular qualities could they have had to equip them to share in his ministry? They seem to have been a close knit group whom Jesus had probably known for some time. But clearly the moment when they decided to leave all and follow him was deeply etched in their memory. Notice how Mark, who was probably writing down Peter's own reminiscences, records the eye-witness detail that Simon and Andrew were casting their nets at the time, whilst James and John were mending theirs. When Jesus said he would make them 'fishers of men', what expertise and experience could they bring to such a task?

Turn now to the second reading for today: John 1.43-51. Here we see how the call was extended to people with other kinds of experience. Only Philip was called by Jesus directly. The others came at the bidding of their friends or families. Yet when they found Jesus for themselves, it was as if he had been searching for them all along. It is the kind of experience which Francis Thompson records in his poem, *The Hound of Heaven*.

> Still with unhurrying chase,
> And unperturbed pace,
> Deliberate speed, majestic instancy,
> Came on the following Feet,
> And a Voice above their beat -
> 'Naught shelters thee, who wilt not shelter Me.'

Like the poet, Nathanael eventually found Christ, only to discover that Christ found him long before he recognized who it was who was pulling at his heart strings.

✳ *Lord, I thank you for those whose influence first led me into your company.*
Show me if there is someone in my immediate circle to whom I should be particularly commending your call.

Day 6   *John 13.1-17*

Serving us

Archbishop William Temple said of this passage, 'We rather shrink from this revelation. We are ready, perhaps, to be humble before God; but we do not want him to be humble in his dealings with us.' We want our heroes to remain on their pedestals, so that we who aspire to be like them may hope one day to share in the honour and privilege they enjoy.

Read this familiar passage very carefully, trying to see it from the point of view of each of the main characters in the story. What do you think this unexpected action of Jesus meant for Peter, for John, for Judas, for Mary (who must surely have been somewhere near her Son on that last evening)? With which of them do you identify yourself most readily?

Christ's humility shows itself in his readiness to serve us. Ours shows in our readiness to receive his service. It is said that it is better to give than to receive. But it is sometimes harder to receive. It puts us in the debt of the one who gives, and robs us of the pride of being in the position of giving to others. Who are the people from whom you receive the most in terms of humble service and menial tasks? How often do you give them the honour they deserve?

* *Won't you let me be your servant,*
  Let me be as Christ to you?
  And pray that I may have the grace
  To let you be my servant too.

Richard Gillard
from The Servant Song (Maranatha, USA)

Day 7   *Mark 10.13-16*

Seeing the Kingdom in the smallest child

The point of this passage goes far beyond an expression of love for the little ones. Nowhere else in the Gospel is Jesus described as 'indignant'. Offence against children always made him angry. The Kingdom belonged to them. Some scholars suggest that verse 15 is a later addition by a scribe, to try to explain why Jesus, unlike most men of his time, took notice of children. The main point of the story is our attitude to them, particularly in their vulnerability. We give them little importance; Jesus sees them as inheritors of the Kingdom. So he publicly blesses them, with gestures in which some commentators see a prefiguring of a later ritual of infant baptism. But whether that is so or not, the story is a stern reminder to us all that children are not 'the church of tomorrow'; they are part of the Church of today. It depends on the witness of that Church as to what kind of tomorrow they will inherit.

* *Lord, save me from any action or word*
  that would put a stumbling block
  in the way of one of your little ones.

Day 8   *1 Corinthians 1.26-31*

The weak and foolish

Paul could hardly be accused of flattering the congregation at Corinth! His words here are spoken partly in anger with people who have become quarrelsome and divided among themselves. He wants to warn them against thinking that they know all there is to know about the faith. But even as he reminds them of their humble origins, it is as if the wonder of what God has done with such simple people overwhelms him, and he sees even their limitations as a sign of God's grace.

We can sometimes harbour romantic illusions about what the Church should be like, a company of saints in shining armour! But then we meet some local congregations and we become disillusioned. It is never a good thing to live with illusions. The reality about the Church is much more splendid. It is among this frail, struggling, sinful community of folk that we find heroes and heroines of the faith who outshine and outshame those whom the world admires for their power, their wealth and their strength. The gospel speaks its word of liberation, not through the powerful but through the oppressed. May God make us humble enough to receive it from them!

✶ *God, who has chosen the weak and the foolish,*
help me to be glad that I am one of them.
Save me from false pretensions or delusions of grandeur
and teach me that your grace is sufficient for me,
that your strength is made perfect in my weakness.

For personal reflection or group discussion

When have you been surprised by Jesus' response to a person or situation? What have you learnt from the moment of surprise?

In what ways do we need to change that others may find the quality of our lives challenging?

ACTION

Think of opportunities you might have to draw others into conversation – in the supermarket, at the hairdressers, taking children to school, on the bus . . . See the passage in John 4.1-6 as a guide.

A LIVING COMMUNITY

Notes on **1 Corinthians** based on the New Jerusalem Bible by

Joseph G Donders

Joseph G Donders, a Dutch Roman Catholic priest ordained in the Society of Missionaries of Africa at Galashiels in Scotland, was formerly Head of the Department of Philosophy and Religious Studies at the State University of Nairobi, Kenya, and Chaplain to the Catholic students there. He now works in Washington DC as Professor of Mission and Cross-cultural Studies at the Washington Theological Union.

Paul insists that the same Spirit is given to all. He remains puzzled by the fact that this Spirit does not keep them together more effectively. At the same time he recognizes that the same Spirit is given in different ways to the different Churches and even to different households and individuals in those Churches. It is variety that makes us into the One we are, something we will only fully realize once we make contact and begin to celebrate our differences together, remembering Jesus, who came 'to gather together into one the scattered children of God' (John 11.52).

Day 9   *1 Corinthians 1.1-9*

You've all got it!

From the beginning of his letter to the Corinthians, Paul wants to offset the remarks people usually make when challenged: 'We can't do that.' 'It is too much for me.' 'We are not yet so far.' It was the difficulty the Reverend Martin Luther King Junior met when he wanted to involve his people in their struggle for human rights. He had to convince them that they could do it. It proved to be the most difficult part of his mission.

It is Paul's message: You are fully equipped. You are not lacking in any spiritual or other gift. You will continue to be strengthened until the end. 'You can rely on God, who has called you to be partners with his Son Jesus Christ our Lord' (verse 9).

✷ *With this faith I will go out and carve a tunnel of hope from a mountain of despair . . .*
With this faith, we will be able to achieve this new day, when all of God's children will . . . be able to join hands and sing '. . . Thank God Almighty we are free at last!'
> Rev. Martin Luther King Jr.,
> April 4 1968, some hours before his violent death. Quoted in
> Candles in the Dark, Mary Craig, (Hodder & Stoughton)

Day 10   *1 Corinthians 1.10-17*

Partnership

Rumours about divisions in Corinth upset Paul. The facts about our divisions would upset him in the same way. The group names on our denominational baptismal membership cards differ from the ones in Corinth. Our separation, because of those names, would baffle Paul. Aren't we all personally connected to one and the same Jesus Christ? Does that connection (or *koinonia*) not imply a vital union among ourselves? Does our division not flaw the intention of Jesus, who came to gather the scattered children of God (John 11. 52)?

If we don't support each other as sisters and brothers, what remains in us of the hope Jesus brought to this world? This hope is a place where we bear each other up in love, and where we share each other's life as sisters and brothers, who in Jesus Christ became friends in the way he became our friend.

✷ *To be a Christian does not mean to be religious in a particular way . . . but a human being – not a type of human being, but the unique person that Christ creates in us. That is metanoia: . . . allowing oneself to be caught up in the way of Jesus Christ.*
> Dietrich Bonhoeffer, July 18 1944, 10 months before his
> execution. Quoted in Candles in the Dark, Mary Craig,
> (Hodder & Stoughton)

Day 11   *1 Corinthians 2.1-5*

God's power

Paul simply states that our faith should depend 'not on human wisdom but on the power of God' (verse 5). The question is where do we find that power? It is not to be found in human wisdom, Paul says. It is not to be found in the reasons people normally use to motivate their behaviour. It is not to be found in our world where, because of the materialistic hardness of our hearts, all seems to be reduced to greed and gain.

God's power is found when that hardness is broken through. We find it every time when a cup of water, or anything else needed, is lovingly given *because of that need*, and because of nothing else.

We see God's power break through when others do this, but also when we catch ourselves acting like that. Those breakthroughs – and they are more frequent than we often guess – are the foundation of our faith. As Paul notes they witness to God's mystery in us! We should witness to them!

✶ *'Human solidarity, as witnessed by any community that welcomes refugees . . . is a source of hope for the real possibility of living together in fraternity and peace.'*

Pontifical Council 'Cor Unum', Refugees: A Challenge to Solidarity, Catholic Truth Society, London 1992.

✶ **Lord God, go on reminding us that any human solidarity shown by others and by ourselves connects us to your love in us.**

Day 12   1 Corinthians 3.1-9

God's farm

The Shorter Oxford Dictionary definition of a 'farm' is 'a tract of land under one management'. That is what Paul says we are, one farm, God's farm. We are a farm on a piece of earth, with plants and animals, depending on sun and rain, worked by women and men with their varied skills and activities. The farm is overlooked by a manager – in this case God – who runs it under one and the same account.

From the first crow of the cock in the morning, to the last rattling of milk cans by farmhands in the evening, a ranch is the result of what nowadays is often called a 'synergy', where all created elements meet and work together to bring forth the results expected.

It asks for a just division of tasks, a continuity of effort, an equitable distribution of the produce, an economy of means, a deep respect for water and light, for seasons and natural cycles, for community, connectiveness and wholeness. Paul does not write that we should live 'as if' we are God's farm. He insists we are that enterprise!

★ **Lord, you gave us the land to provide us with all we need. We thank you for the fruits of the earth. May the power of this saving mystery bring us even greater gifts.**
Adapted from Prayers after a Harvest, from the Roman Missal – the Weekday Missal (Collins Liturgical Publications, London 1982)

Day 13   1 Corinthians 3.10-15

Christ as foundation

You see it sometimes in a field – the foundation of a house and nothing more. The house was never built. Or if it had ever been built, it did not stand the fire of its time. It was destroyed in a conflict or war. The foundation is all that was left. It is lying there as a kind of invitation to start all over again and do a better job.

Paul calls Christ a foundation. That means etymologically that, according to him, Christ lies 'at the bottom' of things. Paul insists that we have to organize those 'things'. Even if we don't do that, the foundation in us will remain our saving force, but our life and what we did with it will go 'through fire'. Nothing of it will be left. And in the end it will become evident to us – what others always thought – that we Christians never managed to build the house in which we ourselves – together with all the others – would feel at home. The foundation is there, and what we have been building on top of it is there for everyone to see! Is it gold, or is it straw they see?

★ **May we live in a manner worthy of our calling, make us witnesses of your truth to all.** *Prayer for Unity from the Roman Missal (Collins Liturgical Publications, London 1982)*

Day 14   1 Corinthians 3.16-23

On bragging

Do not brag, Paul warns us. Those who think themselves wise must learn to be unwise, before they really can be wise. It sounds puzzling. It is simple. We all know of boasters – those who know it all. There is no mystery to them. They do not want to learn anything at all any more. They, Paul implies, are their own worst enemies.

There was a missionary who had been educated at a solid Christian School, the best in the country. He had gone to an Asian country, to bring the good news to the 'unreached'. After his return to home, he was sitting in our circle, and he said, 'I thought I knew it all, till I discovered how they had been walking with God for ages and ages. It was an enriching, but also such a humbling experience.'

Enlarge your circle, says Paul, listen to others, Paul, Peter, Apollos, the world, life and death, the present and the future. They are your servants, they all have something to help you! Don't boast, don't close yourself up in your small circle.

✸ *Lord, you guide creation with parental care, as you have given all of us a common origin. Help us to come together into one family and to keep together in love.*

Adapted from Prayer for Peace and Justice, Roman Missal (Collins Liturgical Publications, London, 1982)

Day 15   1 Corinthians 12.1-11
Gifts
An inter-denominational Church is, of course, sensitive to differences. In Washington DC 'The Church of the Saviour' is such an inter-denominational Church. They are sometimes asked to give account for their type of community. They answer by speaking of the evoking and exercising of gifts. The classes they give in their School of Christian Living, the sermons they preach, the conferences they hold are to help them with the discovery of their gifts.

Like Paul they describe 'Church' as a gift-arousing, gift-bearing community. This description is based on the conviction that when God calls persons, they are called into the fullness of their own potential. That is why, so they say, 'Church' implies a people, a dappled people. Some can heal, others have the gift of reconciling, praying, doing accounts, cooking, sewing, educating or building.

There are no lesser gifts. Each is crucial for the proper functioning of the body. Each contributes to the rich diversity needed by the Church for its work within the total organism of creation. *Adapted from Elizabeth O'Connor, Eighth Day of Creation (Word Books, Waco, Texas)*

✸ *Carry the following biblical proverb with you today:*
 Like clouds and wind that bring no rain is (the one) who boasts of gifts s/he never gives.   Proverbs 25.14 (REB)

For personal reflection or group discussion

- 'To understand others, we must not annex them, but rather make ourselves their guests.' *Louis Massignon*
- Read in all four Gospels one event in the life of Jesus, for example his agony in the garden, or the reason the Gospels give for his death on the cross. How do they compare?

Day 16 *1 Corinthians 12.12-31*

Oneness

We are 'created in the image of God'. It sounds like a secret code that still had to be unravelled, the hidden treasure that still has to be found. Jesus elucidated it when he prayed, 'May they all be one, just as, Father, you are in me and I am in you' (John 17.21). This oneness is so essential that we were not left with some words and a prayer only. We are surrounded by a world that is signalling this truth about ourselves. 'Look at a vine,' Jesus would say, 'we belong together as the branches, the roots and the trunk of a plant.'

'Look at yourself, look at your own body,' Paul writes, 'Don't you see the message it carries? Don't you understand how the very different parts like ears, eyes and nose, hands and feet belong together, and that they would not make any sense – would not even be able to exist, without each other? Don't you hear what your body wants to say about all of us?'

✷ *Prayerfully pay attention to the trees around you, in your street, or those you pass today walking through a park. They deserve the attention Jesus paid to them. They help us understand ourselves, our relationship to God and others.*

Day 17 *1 Corinthians 14.1-12*

Communication

It was after a conference on a religious topic that a friend asked him how it had been. He answered, 'Very helpful, I understood every single word I heard.' He obviously had attended many workshops and conferences where people had been speaking a language he had not caught at all! In this chapter, Paul writes about the need for real communication. Without it, we won't be able to sing a single song. If we don't tune in to each other we will remain like strangers. Paul asks us to develop spiritual gifts that foster communication, improve, encourage and console.

He says this to a Christian community where this communication had been disturbed, like so many of our own polarized congregations, not to speak about the difficulties between different Church communities. The importance of his advice reaches beyond a mere church encounter. It is pertinent to any context where we meet. It is but too easy to go on your own, to get lost in non-communicative small-talk, mystifying everyone else and eventually even yourself!

✴ *Let us be concerned for each other, to stir a response in love and good works. Do not absent yourself from your own assemblies, as some do, but encourage each other.*

Hebrews 10.24-25

Day 18   1 Corinthians 14.13-25

All together

In September 1993, the Second Parliament of the World's Religions met in Chicago. The USA is now home to over 1,500 different religious groups, of which the great majority are of Christian pedigree! The catalogue of major representations numbered over 600 entries and ran to 150 pages.

Any uninitiated unbeliever coming into the meeting must have thought that the speakers, speaking in all kinds of strange tongues were 'mad' – as Paul wrote in the text of today. There was one exception. The 200 assembly's spiritual leaders concluded the sessions deciding to come to the aid of the planet Earth. They all signed a 'Declaration of Global Ethic', condemning poverty, the social disarray of nations and abuses of the earth's eco-systems, and spelling out commitments to a culture of non-violence and respect for life, of solidarity and a just economic order, of tolerance and truthfulness, of equal rights and partnership between men and women.

Paul wrote that if an unbeliever would find everybody prophesying in a religious meeting, he would say, 'God is really among you!' That is what happened in Chicago on that issue!

✴ *Enjoy the earth gently*
Enjoy the earth gently
For if the earth is spoiled
It cannot be repaired
Enjoy the earth gently.   *Yoruba Poem, West Africa*

Day 19   *1 Corinthians 14.26-33*

In turn

Paul asks Christians, who come together to speak in tongues and to prophesy, to do that in turns. They should do this to keep at peace under the direction of God's Spirit. It is something we know from our own experience. The moment two do not listen to each other any more – both at the same time – their mutual love is in danger.

Isn't the most common complaint we hear when a relationship breaks up, 'You don't listen to me! You never listen to me!' In a book that has, for more than eight years, been on the best-sellers list of the New York Times, *A Road Less Traveled*, the psychiatrist Scott Peck does not hesitate to define love as the willingness to listen.

In all Christian Churches God's Spirit is at work. In all of them people prophesy under the influence of that Spirit. Paul suggests that we speak in turn, listen to each other and 'weigh carefully what is said', so that we all may learn, be encouraged and brought together in peace.

✷ *Alleluia, Alleluia!*
May the peace of Christ reign in your hearts,
because it is for this that you were called together
in one body. Alleluia.   *Colossians 3.15*

Day 20   *Haggai 2.1-9*

God's dwelling place

On the twenty-first day of the seventh month Yahweh made it clear to Haggai, the prophet, that God wanted a house, a temple in their midst. God wanted a place where the people would be with their Lord. A place where all the nations of the earth would come together, filling the house with their glory, and realizing peace for all.

The temple Haggai asked for in the name of God is not the end of this story. Later on in the story of the relation between God and the people, Jesus came in, saying of the temple, 'Destroy this sanctuary, and in three days I will raise it up.' John, who tells us this, explained, 'He was speaking of the sanctuary that was his body . . .' (John 2.18-22). Jesus declared himself to be the new sanctuary. His disciples did not immediately understand what he was talking about. They did after he rose among them from the dead. Jesus, the new sanctuary, is the new meeting place where the human and divine meet. Jesus is where we meet God's life, where we are invited to be one with God, and with each other.

✷ *Reflect prayerfully on these words:*
   I believe in God, and God is as God is in Jesus.

David Jenkins

Day 21   *Luke 5.33-39*

Life and growth

It happens all the time. Something new is introduced and immediately the old reacts. The wider the new vision, the stronger the reaction. Examples abound. Think about the ecumenical hopes of the sixties and their meagre results in the nineties, because of the old stifling the vision. Think of the political vision that took on the old nationalisms and the difficulties those deeply rooted sentiments cause.

We have sayings rationalizing all this; 'The more things change the more they remain the same'; 'History repeats itself' – maxims that make any reformation tremble! Jesus faced these human hesitations. People surrounded him because they wanted to change the world and, at the same time, hoped that it would not change too much, that some patching up of the old garment would do. 'Nobody who has been drinking the old wine wants new. "The old is good," he says' (Luke 5.39).

Jesus understood, but he did not agree. He did not agree at all! He discounted patchwork and old wineskins!

✷ ***Prayerfully consider the saying: 'I, God, am your playmate! I will lead the child in you in wonderful ways for I have chosen you.***

Mechtild of Magdeburg, quoted in The Coming of the Cosmic Christ, Matthew Fox (Harper and Row, San Francisco, 1988)

Day 22   *Luke 21.1-6* ✷

Widow's mite

Jon Sobrino, a Central American theologian, in his book *The Hidden Motives of Pastoral Action*, explains that often Gospel stories are not correctly interpreted, but manipulated in view of the church's interest. The usual interpretation of the story of the widow's mite is – according to Sobrino – a good example. She gives everything she has, and Jesus praises her for her generosity. Jesus also does something else. Just before the incident about the widow, Jesus preaches against those scribes 'who devour the property of widows and for show offer long prayers' (20.46-47).

He then sits down in the Temple and sees the widow putting her two coins in the offering box. He praises her, but in this context it comes across as a complaint. A complaint against a Temple, a theology and a priesthood that does not protect a poor widow from doing what she did. How can they tolerate such a woman giving 'all she had to live on'? What kind of caring and sharing community is this?

Leaving the Temple, Jesus tells them that one day it will simply fall apart.

✶ *God of Goodness, you provide for all your creation.*
Give us an effective love for our brothers and sisters,
who suffer from lack of food. Help us to do all we can to
relieve their hunger, that they may serve you with
carefree hearts.
Roman Missal (Collins Liturgical Publications, London 1982)

For personal reflection and group discussion

- Think how you as a community member, and as a worker would be able to help your church community to be involved in the 'gathering of the scattered children of God' (John 11.52).
- Is there any effort in your community at the grassroots level to open the lines of communication with the rest of the Christian world?

ACTION

Have a conversation with someone from a different race, culture, religion or Christian denomination on the hope that lives among us.

BREAD OF LIFE

Notes based on the New English Bible by

Alec Gilmore

Alec Gilmore is a Baptist minister who spent 20 years in pastorates in Northampton and West Worthing after which he exercised a literature ministry for developing countries and Eastern Europe as Director of FEED THE MINDS. He is presently Associate Baptist Chaplain in Brighton and Sussex Universities, and lectures on the Old Testament.

These two weeks lead us from the very practical (bread when you are hungry) to the essentially spiritual (life in Christ) – from a people for whom life is bread to a people for whom Bread is life. Yet the distinction is false. Even in the wilderness bread was a spiritual matter, and even today among the most spiritual the Bread of Life carries material implications. For two weeks allow your mind to pivot on the Bread of Life, swinging to and fro every day from the centre to the material, from the material to the spiritual, and then back to the centre.

---

1. The bread we break

Day 23   Exodus 16.1-15

Hunger pains

It is strange how quickly public mood can change. The previous four chapters saw the death of the first-born, the exodus, the Red Sea crossing and the Triumph Song of Moses. And now, within a matter of weeks, we are plunged into murmurings against the leadership. How could any people have such short memories? But perhaps it says something to us about the power of hunger to warp the mind (the longing to die), to gnaw at the emotions (they idealize even the flesh pots of Egypt, are completely out of touch with what Moses has already achieved and question his motives) and to freeze the will (there seems little attempt to find food for themselves and they are not even very good at recognizing it when it is 'put on a plate' in front of them). This story helps us to appreciate the power of hunger and to begin to understand why desperate people often do strange things. The response of Moses and the Almighty is neither to react to the complaint nor to try to 'understand the problem'. It is to meet the basic need.

✷ *Father, when I meet a hungry person,*
  touch my will to respond before anything else.

Day 24   Exodus 16.16-36

Use and abuse

Don't ask 'how much is an omer?' (about half-a-gallon) or about the conflicting instructions (a precise measure but also 'as much as he can eat') or indeed what manna was (probably a form of honey-dew, the secretion of two kinds of insect, rich in three basic sugars and pectin). What matters is that at the end of the day they had all had enough. Measures and agreements, policies and theories, trade and tariffs all come second compared to meeting basic human need. Concentrate more on the point that, even when their hunger is being met, people who have gone through their experience are still frightened and suspicious – it takes a lot of trust not to 'take thought for tomorrow' especially when sometimes (before the Sabbath) they are told that is exactly what they ought to do. Distinguishing between use and abuse is not always easy in crisis, either for 'purchasers' or for 'providers'. Fortunately, life has its own built-in system of checks and balances. Take too much and it will rot! And always keep one omer special – just as a reminder.

✷ *Father if my first duty is to respond,*
  help me next to distinguish between
  'help' which helps and 'help' which hinders.

Day 25   Psalm 23

Purchasers and providers

In the context of bread and hunger, reflect on the tensions of the sheep rather than the comfort offered by the shepherd. Crucial to the sheep are food and water. In Palestine both are in short supply but what the sheep must find hard is why, when they are at least nibbling at something, they constantly have to be moved by a powerful person with a rod and a staff who always seems to know best. But then sheep are sometimes less aware than they might be of dangers from drinking from a raging torrent, or the enemies that lie in wait in the valleys, or the dangers of getting too close to the edge and falling over. On occasions it is re-assuring to have a kindly hand helping you to water, or pouring oil on a few scars. And you can't have one without the other, so it is largely a matter of settling for a good shepherd whom you can trust, taking the rough with the smooth and trying to understand your provider when things go wrong.

✷ *Lord, the source and giver of life,*
help me to seek you in the tension,
in the light of human suffering and not apart from it.

Day 26   1 Kings 17.8-16

Enough for all

When the story begins there is not sufficient food for the widow and her son. When it ends there is enough for the whole household 'for many days'. Why? Because of Elijah? Yes – because it was his need that brought her need to light. If he had turned up in the village complete with flask and sandwiches, like many tourists in Third World countries, none of it would ever have come to light. Hunger and deprivation often need gentle encouragement to come to the surface.

Because of a miracle? Yes – because humanly speaking there was nothing else that could bring change for these two desperate people. Any solution just had to be a miracle.

But (more than either), there was enough food because of sharing – and not really the sharing of the rich with the poor or the 'haves' with the 'have-nots', but the sharing of those who have little with those who have even less.

✷ *Father, take away the pride*
that prevents me from admitting my need
and lead me to the person who has a similar need
so that together we may find in you the Bread of Life.

Day 27   Proverbs 9.1-11

A call to live

Proverbs bridges the gap between provision of basic necessities and a different quality of living.

Imagine a wise woman (Wisdom) inviting her friends to a banquet. She is rich – her house has seven pillars, she has beasts to slaughter, wine to drink, maids to deliver the invitations. Truly a 'provider', a shepherd with some potential and perhaps not too many needs to worry about. Notice whom she invites – 'the simple' (verse 4). The word is variously translated as 'fool', 'simpleton', 'ignorant' or even 'open-minded' but usually has a tendency to the bad rather than the good. Whether they are her normal clientele may be left to the imagination but the impression we are left with is that they are the sort of people who are normally avoided (Cf. Luke 14.15-24).

Notice what she offers. 'Live' (verse 6) suggests participation in 'true life' rather than continuity of physical existence and verses 7-11 fill out the detail, focusing on insight, understanding and respect for God.

✲ *Father, when I am busy sharing my needs*
  and responding to the needs of others
  help me never to take my eye off my need for eternal life,
  and always keep me aware
  that the two could be the same.

Day 28   Isaiah 55.1-13
True worth

Think of these verses as being addressed to a people who are desperate. They have been living in exile for years and have little prospect of return. They have no money and when they get any they spend it on all the wrong things. Isaiah is less concerned with their current plight than with their future possibilities. He wants to give them hope based on the fact that God loves them – he has chosen them and glorified them.

How can they achieve their true worth? It must begin with repentance, both negative ('forsake') and positive ('seek' and 'return'), because of the gap between the life they are leading and the life God has for them. After that it is not so much a matter of effort as of trust and patience. God's word has its own power, even if it is often slow to bring change, like snow and rain effecting change on the earth. But for those who trust there is a new future – out of exile into a different world – and for those in every generation who find themselves in the same situation.

✲ *Father, give me this bread of life*
  that I may hunger no more.

Day 29   *Acts 2.41-47*

All things common

Once the early Christians discover what it is that holds them together (their common life in Christ) it is but a short step to fulfil some of the ancient prophecies. The breaking of bread in the Old Testament, as a sign of God's will that his people should be one, now manifests itself as an expression of the unity already achieved. The breaking of bread in the Old Testament as the first obligation of charity, and as a way of making peace with the person with whom it was shared, now finds fulfilment in the sharing of all things, because all members of the community are at peace with one another. For one brief moment in church history the material and the spiritual go hand-in-hand. The new life creates the sharing and the sharing is the life. Too readily we dismiss it as an early and failed attempt at 'communism', instead of seeing it as an indictment in the past and a pointing forward to what one day might be.

✳ *Lord, when I even so much as glimpse your ideal, give me the courage to go for it, and make my ears deaf to those who would hold me back.*

For personal reflection or group discussion

1. Identify one or two groups of people who are in desperate straits (not necessarily the result of hunger or poverty) and ask yourself how much allowance you can make for the peculiar and often stupid things they do. If you know someone who works with such people ask them to help you understand their unusual behaviour.

2. A mark of good people is that they share their bread with the stranger (Isaiah 58.7) and even with the enemy (Proverbs 25.21 and Romans 12.20). Reflect on how much time you spend eating and drinking with strangers or with people you find it difficult to get on with.

3. Try reading *How The Other Half Dies, The Real Reasons for World Hunger*, Susan George (Penguin Books, 1976) or *Rural Development. Putting the Last First*, Robert Chambers (Longman, Scientific and Technical, 1983). Ask yourself all the time how far charity really helps, and make a list of those qualities which demonstrate the true worth of people struggling in Third World countries.

2. Bread broken for us

We move from the provision of food and water as evidence of God's power and concern and from the sharing of bread as an expression of our common humanity to a fuller exploration of the new life in Christ – not the 'bread we break' but the 'bread broken for us'. We explore the divisions that exist even in a caring and sharing society (Romans and Corinthians). We discover that there is more to life than material things (food) and that sometimes that 'something more' has to do with attitude and feeling rather than theory and action.

Day 30   1 Corinthians 11.23-29
Class division

For the church at Corinth, the division had less to do with the hungry and the satisfied and more with social and class division. If we relate these words to our local church they may not seem relevant. But on the world stage, not only are some churches richer than others but even the same Church will be rich in one continent and poor in another as Christians help themselves instead of 'sharing bread'. Paul sees this as a denial of the life in Christ.

For him, first, the regular 'sharing of bread' is a symbol which began literally with the 'breaking of the body' and recognition of this is the first step to healing.

Second, never must they share the bread without remembering it – and not only 'as often as we celebrate the sacrament' but every time we partake of our daily bread.

Third, even to remember is to take a step in the healing process. So a spiritual act brings about a material result and a material result brings about a spiritual healing.

✷ *Father, may I never eat without remembering*
   those from whom I am separated
   and, as I remember, show me what to do
   so that I may begin the process of healing.

Day 31   *Romans 14.10-23*

Race division

In Rome the division was between Jew and Gentile and one unpleasant aspect of it was judgmental attitudes as between the 'strong' and the 'weak'. The strong were those who could eat anything, handle anything, cope with anything, had all the answers, and lacked nothing in confidence. The 'weak' were those who felt all kinds of limitations and endeavoured to live within them. You might say the strong were those who were proud of their culture and had taken steps to convince others of their superiority. The weak were embarrassed by theirs and had always been made to feel inferior, like fish constantly being told by birds that there is something superior about flying!

Paul pleads with the strong not to be critical of the weak on the grounds that such behaviour is hurtful and offensive. More important than what is right and wrong is what helps (or hinders) our brother growing up in love. But then is it not that which makes something right or wrong? And is not true strength (15.1) fulfilling our obligation to support the weak rather than condemning them?

✳ *Lord, when I feel weak give me strength,*
and when I feel strong keep me humble.

Day 32   *John 6.22-27*

Not by bread alone

Verses 22-24 are somewhat confusing but the details are not important. Three things stand out.

First, on the day after Jesus fed the five thousand, the people are determined to stay with him. Confused they may be and their motives questionable but this man has something and they have no intention of missing it. Their enthusiasm, determination and single-mindedness all indicate their hunger.

Second, Jesus is not confused. What he had done the day before was to give them food because they were hungry – no more and no less! But today they are not pursuing him because they are hungry but because they believe (or hope) he has superhuman powers. But they must not imagine that his provision of food in the wilderness is going to herald the arrival of the Kingdom of God.

Third, Jesus wants them to see that there is something else they ought not to miss. His Kingdom may include food provision but that is not what it is about.

* *Lord, when I am obsessed with the material
help me to perceive the spiritual within,
and when I am carried away by the spiritual
put my feet back on the ground.*

Day 33   John 6.28-40

What else?

People who are activity-driven (as the Jews in these verses were) find it hard in a world where 'doing' may not be what matters. So instinctively, their response to the suggestion that there is a spiritual equivalent to 'earning your bread' is 'what do we have to do to get it?'(verse 27). For Jesus the answer is simple. Believe in him and his way of life. 'Being' may be more important than 'doing'; attitude and feelings come before actions and theories.

But can he do what Moses did? The manna made people believe. Jesus says it wasn't Moses who provided it. It was his Father. And just as his Father had given them physical bread in the wilderness to satisfy physical hunger, so now his Father is giving spiritual food to meet a spiritual need in the person of Jesus. (Notice the careful change of tense in verse 32: 'gave' becomes 'gives'.) But it is too much for them. They cannot recognize him. They are missing out on what God is giving because they are too tied to something he gave once before.

* *Lord, prevent me from being so committed to the past that I am unable to recognize you in the present.*

Day 34   John 6.41-51

Jesus 'on the ropes'

Objection! This time Jesus has gone too far with his claim to be the Bread of Life. They know him. They know where he came from. How dare he? Under pressure to defend his claims, the arguments Jesus puts forward are not exactly the clearest. He reminds them that according to their own teaching a man can only believe if God instructs him (verses 44-45), which seems something of a circular argument (almost a 'Catch 22 situation'). He then goes further, and suggests that it is not his business simply to engage in short-term solutions that will stay a person's hunger for a day, but to provide Bread (i.e. his flesh and blood) for the life of the world. And so a new dimension is added. No longer are we talking about emergency rations – short-term solutions or acts of love and charity – but about nothing less than a totally different way of life. In short, a revolution! And like many other revolutions, it begins to look as if it could start with an assassination.

✷ *Lord, sometimes I find it difficult
to see where you are going
but please give me grace to keep following.*

Day 35   *John 6.52-59*
No other way

The idea of 'eating his flesh' was probably no more readily understood by his hearers then than by his readers now, whilst the further suggestion of 'drinking his blood' would be outrageous to every Jew. Jesus, having stuck his neck out, now proceeds to lay it down upon a block! They may find what he says puzzling and what he advocates offensive, but there is no other way to the sort of life he is putting before them. Providing food is not the answer. A different life-style is. In these verses we have moved from the charitable to the sacramental – from one who is prepared to provide bread to one who is prepared to give his life. And if everyone knows that without bread a person dies – and many would say that if we are unwilling to provide bread something of the 'human' in us dies also – Jesus goes further when he says that without sharing fully in the life he offers, the fully human is not even born.

✷ *Lord, forgive me
if I find it easier to see you in material things
than in the spiritual,
and please help me to move more easily
through one to the other and back again, as you did.*

Day 36   *Luke 24.28-35*
Our daily bread

Jesus had told them that whenever they passed round the bread and cup they were to remember him. And they were remembering. They had been remembering all the way along the road. But they were not seeing. 'Bread to eat' and 'the Bread of Life' were still in separate compartments – material and spiritual – until the familiar act of breaking the bread, and 'the penny dropped'. Discovering the spiritual in the material is learning to recognize the significance of the ordinary, to remove a layer and penetrate a depth, rather like noticing and learning to appreciate something you have lived with for years and never even noticed, like paint on walls, a tree on the highway, or the ground you walk on. Or suddenly recognizing human need that you have lived with for years and never seen, perhaps because you have met one or two people personally who are committed to meeting it, perhaps because you have actually met one or two of their clients, or maybe because you have felt that same need yourself. On the surface, and to others, it may all look just as material as it ever did, but to you it is different. Your attitude has changed. This is our 'daily bread' – not just food, but life, and vision.

✳ *Lord, open my eyes today, that I may see.*

For personal reflection or group discussion

1. Make a list of the things in your home that you rarely notice, and write alongside each something that strikes you when you stop to look at it. You have removed a layer and become alive in a new way.

2. Choose something in your home that is precious. In a fire you would want to grab it. Why? Reflect on its associations: people, places, memories, emotions and attitudes. As it moves you to thanksgiving, intercession or confession the material becomes the vehicle of the spiritual.

ACTION

Choose someone whom you scarcely know and / or someone whom you find it difficult to get on with and invite him / her to a meal at home or take him / her out to coffee.

LENT – THE WAY OF SUFFERING

Notes based on the New Jerusalem Bible by

Sheila Cassidy

Sheila Cassidy is a medical doctor who has worked for many years with men and women dying of cancer. Her writing is much influenced by this involvement with suffering people and by her own experience of torture, solitary confinement and imprisonment in Chile in 1975. She works in Plymouth General Hospital as a specialist in Palliative Care. In her spare time she preaches, lectures, broadcasts, writes books, and cares for an increasing family of teddy bears!

Towards the end of Luke 9, the evangelist writes of Jesus that 'he resolutely turned his face towards Jerusalem.' In this key phrase he sets the scene for Jesus' journey towards his death. It is a journey which has taken him both physically and emotionally up hill and down dale until at last he goes up to Jerusalem. Here in the Holy City he is initially greeted as the long awaited Messiah. Then comes the all too familiar story: the people turn against him, he is charged, found guilty, and sentenced to death. We have three weeks to walk this journey with Jesus, to try to understand just a little better the life and death of this amazing man who we believe to be the Son of God.

Day 37   Luke 13.34-35
1 Thessalonians 2.1-8

Jesus weeps over Jerusalem

Jesus is muttering anxiously over the Holy City as if he were a mother hen calling her wayward chicks. 'Jerusalem, Jerusalem,' he groans, 'why won't you listen to me, why have you abandoned God, you who were to be God's bride, his beloved people?'

What are we to make of this feminine side of Jesus and why do we so often ignore it? What is it about our understanding of God that makes our projections almost exclusively male?

Jesus, the historical Jesus, of course, was male. That's the way it happened. But, it seems to me, that it could have been otherwise. Had the date of the incarnation been set for say 1980, might not God have sent a daughter, a beloved child, made in his / her own image, to El Salvador or Somalia? Could this child of God not have saved the world by being raped and shot in the back of a white transit van on a bleak hillside outside San Salvador, like my friend Ita Ford, whose mothering of orphans was seen to be a threat to the security of the State?

Jesus wept for the stupidity of the people of Jerusalem as mothers have always wept for their wayward sons and daughters, for mothering and weeping are divine qualities which have been woven into our human fabric because we are crafted in God's image.

✱ *Jesus Lord, Son of God,*
soak our arid hearts with the tears of your compassion.
Give us, too, your awe-full gift of sharing others' pain.

Day 38   Luke 18.31-34

Breaking bad news

How can you soften the news that someone is going to die? Do you tell it straight, like it is, and watch people's faces crumble incredulously as their world disintegrates? Or do you wrap it up in euphemisms, pious platitudes, in the hope – unconscious of course – that the fuse is long enough for you to escape before the explosion, so you won't have to pick up the pieces? Is that what Jesus did, I wonder? I think it was. He *could* have said, 'Look, they're going to arrest me and kill me in Jerusalem, but I've got to go all the same: God wants it of me. I'm going to die: die! Do you understand?' But he didn't do it that way. He talked about the prophets and the mysterious Son of Man: no wonder they didn't understand. After all, they were only simple men, not rabbis, not well read in the scriptures.

And what did the disciples think about it all later, as they sat in the upper room? Did some of them wish that they *had* understood so that they could have supported him better during those terrible last days? That's the trouble, of course, with wrapping up the bitter truth: one person always ends up – alone – facing fear, and his or her friends feel guilty for ever.

✻ *Lord Jesus – the Way, the Truth, the Life –
teach us to love your truth,
however much it hurts.*

Day 39   Luke 18.35-43; cf. Mark 10.46-52

The healing of Bartimaeus

O blind Bartimaeus! You were a lucky fellow: there at just the right moment when Jesus was going past, and in the mood to heal you! What if you'd caught him on another day, before his 'hour' had come, or if your faith hadn't been so strong that it impressed him?

Jesus was always moved by strong faith: the centurion, the woman with the haemorrhage, the man who had himself let down through the roof; they were all cured. But what about the others we never hear about? And what about the people today: all those who go with such faith to healing services and still come out in their wheelchairs, or on their crutches, or blind as bats. If we're honest about it, the psalmist spoke the truth when he said, *'The Lord does whatever he wills.'* God is God, unknowable, all powerful, and we don't really understand him or her at all. The Lord is compassionate, slow to anger and rich in mercy: sure. And Jesus said, 'Ask and it shall be given to you, knock and the door will be opened.' But the fact is, God is not a magician to be bribed, and prayer is not a spell that can be guaranteed to work. God is not like that. Always, always, we're up against the mystery, breaking our necks like birds on the one-way glass through which we see but darkly. But that doesn't mean we should stop asking, throwing our prayers like stones to wake the sleeping baker, to shatter the reinforced glass.

✻ *Jesus Christ, Son of God,
stop, and hear our cry.
We are blind, lame, and sick at heart.
Come, and make us whole.*

Day 40   Luke 19.29-44

Jesus enters Jerusalem

As he nears the city, Jesus sends one of his disciples on a strange mission: to borrow a donkey for him to ride into

Jerusalem. It must have been an amazing sight: the crowd cheering Jesus astride a frisky beast, bucking and snorting – for the colt had never been ridden. This was no surreptitious entry of a man who knew the authorities were out to get him, but a piece of deliberate theatre, a show designed to bait the authorities and pull the crowds.

Was this *really* what happened, I wonder, or did the evangelist write it this way to show that Zechariah's messianic prophecy was being fulfilled:

'Rejoice heart and soul, daughter of Zion!
Shout for joy, daughter of Jerusalem!
Look, your king is approaching,
he is vindicated and victorious,
humble and riding on a donkey,
on a colt, the foal of a donkey.' (Zechariah 9.9)

I like to think that this is how it happened. As he neared his 'hour', his death, Jesus' realization that he was the Messiah was becoming wonderfully and terrifyingly clear. In his entry into Jerusalem, he deliberately acts out the prophecy of the humble Messiah, the servant king, and for the first time accepts as his due the homage of the rejoicing crowd.

✷ *Gentle Messiah, Servant King, humble God,*
we worship you.

Day 41 *Hebrews 5.1-10*
The humanity of the priests
It is around 67BC, some thirty-four years since Jesus died, and an Old Testament scholar of the Diaspora, probably an Alexandrian Jew, writes of priesthood. I find his description wonderfully wise and tender, for though he makes it clear that the priest is chosen by God for the role of intercessor, he dwells more upon human weakness than upon priestly holiness. The priest 'lives in the limitations of weakness': he may eat too much, drink too much, smoke too much, or love unwisely. He is chosen from among his fellow men and women, not because he is holier than they, but so that he who represents may understand them as they deserve to be understood.

Jesus is the prototype of the 'modern' priest, the priest of the new covenant, and the author of Hebrews writes movingly, not of his strength but of his struggle to obey. Through his eyes we glimpse, not the well groomed pastor in his immaculate clericals, but a man weeping by his bedside, crying out in anguish, as priests have before and since: Lord, I can't do it. I can't. I can't. Then, through God's strength comes capitulation, abandonment.

✷ *Lord, if I must, if you want it, I will.*
It is through this suffering, this obedience, this love that we are healed.
Gentle Messiah, Servant King, humble God, we worship you.

Day 42 *Hebrews 10.1-10*
True worship

The need for ritual must lie very deep in the human psyche, even if its form changes as the years go by. It's easy for us to wrinkle our noses in a superior sort of way at the thought of burnt offerings: those terrible ritual barbecues in which beasts were burned – feet, entrails and all. The truth, if we admit it, is that we have exchanged all this for Corpus Christi processions, High Mass and Cathedral evensong. Is God more pleased with the sound of fifty golden haired choir boys than the blood of fifty oxen? I don't really know.

What I do know, however, is what the prophets said again and again about hypocrisy in worship:

'What are your endless sacrifices to me,' says Yahweh?
'I am sick of burnt offerings . . .
You may multiply your prayers, I shall not be listening . . .
Cease to do evil. Learn to do good,
search for justice, discipline the violent,
be just to the orphan, plead for the widow.' (Isaiah 1.11-17)

This theme is taken up again in Amos 5.21 and, of course, by Jesus himself who quoted angrily from Hosea 6.6 when he said to the Pharisees, 'Go and learn the meaning of the words "mercy is what pleases me, not sacrifice"' (Matthew 9.13). Perhaps today he would say, 'Can't you understand that I don't give a fig for your perfect liturgies unless those who offer them love my people? Who asked you to trample in my courts? Go away and shelter the homeless, feed your hungry, comfort your widows, and only then, I'll listen to your hymns and anthems.'

✷ *Lord, I am not worthy to enter your house.*
Give me, I pray, clean hands and an open heart.

Day 43   *Lamentations 1.1-14*

Lament for Jerusalem

The footnote in my Bible tells me that in the Greek version of Lamentations, there is an introductory note: 'When Israel had been taken into captivity and Jerusalem had become a desert, it happened that the prophet Jeremiah sat down in tears: he uttered this lamentation over Jerusalem, he said:

> "O how deserted she sits,
> the city once thronged with people!
> Once the greatest of nations,
> she is now like a widow . . ." '

The Cathedral lies in ruins, a bomb crater where the altar once stood. Stray cats pick their way between shards of stained glass and a widow sits moaning beside the body of her son.

At last, the guns are silent: the time for resistance has passed. The daughters of the city weep in shame, violated by their conquerors, their garments in shreds.

Who weeps for us, Jeremiah?
Who will weep for Beirut, Mogadishu, Sarajevo?
Will we never learn?

✻ *Lord Jesus Christ, you wept for Jerusalem,*
you weep for us.
Forgive the way we abuse your gifts,
forgive us, Lord, forgive us.

For personal reflection or group discussion

Reflect on your own experience if you suffer, or think of someone you know who is suffering. Think of an area of the world where there is immense suffering. What difference does it make to know that God suffers with us?

Day 44   *Luke 20.9-19*

Jesus upsets the Pharisees

After his flamboyant entry into Jerusalem, Jesus begins his last 'mission' to the Holy City. As if allowing himself to be hailed as Messiah were not enough, he causes a terrible scene in the Temple, driving the traders and money lenders out of his 'Father's house'. Is it any wonder then, that the Pharisees are outraged?

It is not difficult to imagine them sitting tight-lipped, just waiting to catch him out. But how can they fault this man whose doctrine is based on their own scriptures? Much as it infuriates them to have the tiresome words of the prophets spelt out to them, they can hardly complain. Then Jesus tells a story about a landlord whose tenants turned against him and they know that he is getting at *them*. Do the ordinary people understand the story? Possibly not, but the Pharisees are scholars, well used to this method of teaching, and they know that Jesus is threatening their whole regime, their corrupt tenure of God's vineyard. Their fingers itch to lay hands on him, but they fear a riot, so they go away to plot in secret, as corrupt men and women have done since time began.

✷ *Lord God, who sees into the hearts of all,*
remind us that we have no secrets from you.
Give us courage to be honest in all our dealings,
to short-change no-one, to pay our taxes gladly.
For you, O Lord, are the God of truth and justice,
and we wish to be like you.

Day 45   Isaiah 56.1-8

The dangers of Pharisaism

It must have been hard for the elders among the Jews, so convinced of their own righteousness, to even contemplate that others might take their place. In their attitude we see the roots of all the 'isms' to which humankind is prey: racism, patriotism, ageism, elitism . . . Perhaps Pharisaism is the great weakness of religious people, all of us who secretly fancy that we are holier than the next woman or man. How can we be so stupid! Do we not remember that Jesus came to call not the just but sinners? Have we not read the story of the Good Samaritan, and understood that it was the orthodox holy people who passed by the wounded man and the outsider who rescued him?

Sometimes it seems to me that my endless failure of love and truth are in reality a precious gift, reminding me that I am no better than my ancestors. Perhaps it is not just material riches that make us too fat to pass through the eye of God's needle; we become even more bloated by pride when we think ourselves completely virtuous. Our God is a God of paradox, a God of surprises, and loves not so much the spiritually rich who tell him about all their continence, their fasting and almsgiving but the sinner who creeps into the back of the church on a

Wednesday night and says, 'O Lord, I've made a mess of my life. I'm sorry. Please help me to do better.'

✽ **Lord of the broken, Lord of the poor,
please leave your door unlocked for 'the foolish virgin' and the late comer.**

Day 46   Luke 22.1-6
The great betrayal

Is there nothing new under the sun? A group of men sit around a table, discussing how they can get rid of someone whom they see as a threat to the security of the comfortable status quo. Should they blackmail him? Destroy his character? Or would it be easier for everyone if he were to have an unfortunate accident? They argue. The phone rings. The leader answers, the others talk quietly among themselves. He puts the phone down and smiles. The others look expectant: 'Gentlemen, I think we have a solution to our problem . . .'

O Judas, Judas! What came over you? Was it just the money, or was there more to it than that?

✽ **Lord, we pray for all who betray their friends:
for all who betray the trust of little children,
    by violence or abuse;
for men and women led by boredom, foolishness or
    lust to break their marriage vows;
for clergy everywhere who preach one way and live
    another.
Forgive them, Lord;
and forgive us, for we too betray your trust and love.**

Day 47   Luke 22.7-23
The last supper

Scholars tell us that the cup Jesus passes among his disciples as they share the Passover wine in fellowship is set in deliberate contrast to the cup with which he institutes the Eucharist: 'This cup is the new covenant in my blood poured out for you.' Just as the early Jewish priests endowed an ancient nomad feast with an entirely new significance, so Jesus takes the Passover and names it as a memorial of his death. The scripture parallels are clear: the Israelites were saved by the blood of a sacrificed lamb splashed on their door posts, while we of the new covenant are sayed by the blood of God's Son poured out upon the cross.

'Do this,' he is saying, 'break bread, bless wine, in memory of me. Commemorate in this symbolic act the fact that I lived and spoke the truth, and was killed because of it.'

Sometimes, it seems to me, we lose sight of what we are celebrating. We remember the death all right, we paint pictures, sing hymns, and make ourselves ritually sick and sad: but of what use is this if we forget *why* Jesus died, and fail to make our whole lives a commemoration of his?

✷ *Lord, give us the strength and discipline*
to feed upon your Word,
for how else can we know how you lived and taught?
How else can we claim to be your disciples?

Day 48   Luke 22.24-30
The last shall be first

Jesus delighted in turning things upside down, especially old fashioned, pompous customs in which the rich and powerful lorded it over the poor. The New Testament abounds in stories in which the mighty are tumbled from their thrones and the humble are exalted. Jesus' whole life, his teaching and his concept of Messiah were built upon these 'Magnificat' values. We see it in the story of the publican whose prayer was better heard than that of the Pharisee, in the generosity of the widow with her small gift and in the story of the adulterous woman whose many sins were forgiven.

How exasperated Jesus must have been at that last family supper party when his disciples began to squabble as to which of them was the greatest. Had they not listened to a word he'd said during those three years of teaching? Had they *not seen* how he, like his Father, had consistently favoured the little people? What more could he do? Perhaps it was at this point that Jesus took off his outer garment, wrapped a towel around his waist and began to wash the disciples' feet.

Sometimes, I think, we are like those stupid men, forgetting Jesus' message and always trying to move higher up the ladder of prestige. If we were logical, we'd all be fighting for the chance to serve at table and to do the washing up!

✴ *Lord Jesus, washer of feet,*
give us wisdom to serve your suffering people
with tenderness and humility.

Day 49 *Luke 22.31–38*

The gift of courage

Poor Simon Peter! How well I understand his longing to be brave, to be a hero, to be faithful to his Lord. I too have longed to have courage like Joan of Arc, like Archbishop Romero, like so many of my friends in Latin America, yet found myself very much afraid in the face of hardship and threat to life. For me, however, as for Peter, there came a moment when I found the courage to hold fast, to suffer, to bear witness. There came a day when I was *given* the strength to live with terror, to remain silent under torture, so that I might protect my friends.

I now know the meaning of Paul's statement that we are but earthen vessels (2 Corinthians 4.7), holding the sparkling wine which is our life in God. What is asked of most of us is that we cherish that life, that we keep alive the flame of the spirit which wavers and splutters within us. If we are faithful in all the little things of life – generous, and kind, with a modicum of self discipline – then, I believe, when the moment of testing and challenge comes, we will find ourselves drawing upon reserves of faith, strength and courage that we did not know were there. Planted in the house of the Lord, our roots creep deeper and deeper in the dark earth until they tap into that great underground stream which fed Peter, Paul and all the martyrs and saints.

✴ *Lord Jesus Christ, God of Gethsemane,*
teach us to trust you,
to know that you will give us courage when we need it –
but not before.

Day 50 *Luke 22.39-53*

Jesus in Gethsemane

'Lord! Father, please . . . I can't drink this. I can't face it. It's too bitter. You're asking too much. I'm so afraid. Please, please, take it away.' Whose prayer is this? Yours? Mine? My neighbour's? It is, of course, the prayer of Every man, of men with cancer, women with AIDS, political prisoners facing torture, the girl about to be raped on a lonely heath. It is the prayer of Jesus as he knelt weeping in the garden, so scared that the sweat ran off him like blood.

This is such an important passage, because it confirms for us the humanity of Jesus. Here was no ethereal figure walking to meet his torturers with a serene smile and hands outstretched, but a real man, utterly terrified, begging to be spared the pain and humiliation of torture, the terrible finality of death. But there is something else: Jesus was afraid, begged to be spared, yes: but he added the rider which distinguishes the martyrs from the endless ranks of those who meet violent deaths. He said to God, 'If you want this of me, if it is your will, then take me. I am yours.' It is this simple act of abandonment which shakes the stars in their firmament, which transforms a tragic murder into an act of glory. And we, like Paul, make up in our own poor flesh that which is 'lacking' in the sufferings of Christ. It is only in this mystical economy that we can find any meaning in our own suffering and that of those we love.

✷ *Living God, suffering, fearful God –*
sharing so deeply in our poor humanity –
you have shown us it is all right to be afraid,
because we too are only human.

For personal reflection or group discussion
How do we recognize when it is necessary to hold on and struggle against suffering, and when to let go?

Day 51   Luke 22.54-71
Peter betrays his master
Once, while on retreat, I drew this scene, one of the most poignant in the Passion story. The focus is again on the wretched Peter who, having crept through the darkened courtyards to within perhaps yards of where Jesus is being interrogated by the elders, is sitting by the fire. His heart is in turmoil. What is happening? Why wouldn't the master let the disciples defend him? Why hadn't they all put up a fight? Why had Jesus gone so quietly? What was going on?

As I drew the weeping Peter, sitting slumped on a bench outside the courtyard, I sensed the presence of Jesus and suddenly there he was in my picture, chained, on his way to Golgotha, but standing by Peter's side with his arm around the heaving shoulders. We're not told it was so, but I'm sure that Jesus entered that hollow anguish in Peter's heart, forgiving him and empowering him to move on. I'm sure too, that when we weep for our sins, for our betrayal of God, that somehow Christ is there, his arm around our shoulders, urging us to look forward rather than back, to accept the forgiveness offered so that we can move on to do his work.

✷ *Lord, Jesus Christ, Suffering Servant,*
Lonely God, we weep with Peter
for the many times we have betrayed you.
Like him, we hear the cock crow
and we yearn for your forgiveness.

Day 52   Luke 23.1-12

Jesus before Pilate

What was going on inside Jesus' mind and heart during these two periods of interrogation before Pilate and then Herod? Why did he not answer them, I wonder? Why did he not denounce the chief priests and elders as the whited sepulchres they were and proclaim his gospel of truth and love? Was he cowed by it all, trembling with fear, tongue-tied? And what would we think of him if he were? Why do we always assume that the hero is without fear, that martyrs go to their death with a merry and edifying quip for the onlookers? Life is not like that. Courageous soldiers wet themselves in battle, weep with fear, and then die rescuing a wounded comrade from the line of fire.

I suspect it doesn't really matter *why* Jesus held his tongue. The evangelists make it apparent that during these last days he had an ever increasing sense of his own destiny as the non-violent Messiah, the man of sorrows who allowed himself to be led like a lamb to the slaughter, who in bearing our sins became the instrument of our salvation. Perhaps once he had entered into this role he could do nothing but play it out to the finish, to its terrible, unthinkable end.

This, it seems is the way with brave men. They are afraid, they weep, for themselves and for their loved ones, but somehow, when the moment comes, they hold their heads erect until the weakness of the flesh overcomes the fire of the spirit and they crumble and fall. Alas, we can only speculate as to what Jesus was thinking during those last terrible hours.

Perhaps the words which the Lutheran pastor Dietrich Bonhoeffer wrote as he awaited execution by the Nazis can give us a glimpse into the hidden psycho-spiritual world of those facing death:

* *Who am I? They often tell me*
  I would step from my cell's confinement
  calmly, cheerfully, firmly,
  like a squire from his country house.

  Who am I? They often tell me
  I would talk to my warders
  freely and friendly and clearly,
  as though it were mine to command.

  Who am I? They also tell me
  I would bear the days of misfortune
  equably, smilingly, proudly,
  like one accustomed to win.

  Am I really all that which other men tell of?
  Or am I only what I know of myself,
  restless and longing and sick, like a bird in a cage,
  struggling for breath, as though hands were
  compressing my throat,
  yearning for colours, for flowers, for the voices of birds
  thirsting for words of kindness, for neighbourliness,
  trembling with anger at despotisms and petty humiliation,
  tossing in expectation of great events,
  powerlessly trembling for friends at an infinite distance,
  weary and empty at praying, at thinking, at making
  faint, and ready to say farewell to it all?

  Who am I? This or the other?
  Am I one person today, and tomorrow another?
  Am I both at once? A hypocrite before others,
  and before myself a contemptible woebegone weakling?
  Or is something within me still like a beaten army,
  fleeing in disorder from victory already achieved?

  Who am I? They mock me, these lonely questions of mine.
  Whoever I am, thou knowest, O God, I am thine.

From Letters and Papers from Prison, Dietrich Bonhoeffer (SCM 1971)

Day 53   *Luke 23.13-25*

The violence of the mob

Poor vacillating Pilate: so weak that he let the crowd persuade him to condemn Jesus to death. But what would we have done? Luke tells us that the shouts of the people grew louder and louder, their lust for blood becoming a frenzy. Would we have had the courage to oppose them, to set Jesus free? I hope we would, but I'm not at all sure. I find peaceful crowds intimidating enough, so an angry crowd must be a terrifying sight. The power of mob violence is well known: think of the 'Cristal Nacht', that terrible night when a German crowd ran amok and destroyed the Jewish synagogues until the broken glass lay glinting on the ground like diamonds. Where does this evil force come from, this power for destruction which must surely be greater than the sum of the anger of the individuals present? If ever I were to believe in a mysterious demonic force, I would see it as that which converts a crowd of ordinary citizens into a howling, destructive mob. No. I don't blame Pilate. He must have been scared sick that the crowd would turn on him, tear *him* limb from limb. How near did he come, I wonder, to changing the course of history, of being remembered as the Roman Governor who died trying to save the gentle Messiah from being lynched by the crowd?

Poor Pilate: so near but yet so far. Nearly a hero, but not quite. Your story is our story, isn't it?

✳ *Lord Jesus Christ: we pray for strength to speak your truth,*
to be a voice for the oppressed,
a champion for the poor.
But we are very much afraid for ourselves and our families.
Lord, please help us.

Day 54   *Luke 23.26-43*

Jesus dies on the cross

'When they reached the place called The Skull, there they crucified him . . .' Just like that. One throw-away line: when they climbed up the hill, they killed him, killed the Son of God. Is this brief, obscene act really the pivot on which our world turns, the cornerstone of our faith? Although I was born and bred a Christian, I still find the significance of the crucifixion mind-boggling.

It's not that I don't believe it happened: I have seen far too much violence to doubt the material truth of it all. What I find hard to cope with is the mystery behind the act. I suppose what I am up against is the mystery of the Trinity and the terrible, awesome truth that the God who made us loved us so much that he took on our flesh and all that goes with it, including a terrifying, agonizing death. It's all too much. The only fitting response is silence and tears.

* *Sit for a while in silence.*

Day 55   Luke 23.44-56
Death and new life

In 1980, a friend of mine, a Maryknoll missionary sister called Ita Ford was murdered by the security forces in El Salvador. The following day, or perhaps it was the day after, her body and those of two companions were found in a shallow grave by the roadside. The disinterment of the bodies, in the presence of the American Consul was filmed and had been incorporated into a film called *Roses in December*, alongside the life and death of Jean Donovan, a young lay missionary who worked with Ita in caring for refugee children.

I have watched this film many times, with different groups of people and each time it seems a little harder to watch my friend's body being dragged from the grave with ropes. It seems impossible to believe that only two days before, these pitiful corpses were laughing, vibrant human beings. How narrow is the thread upon which our life hangs, how impenetrable the veil through which we must pass.

Sometimes I think that the passage from this life into the next is like the jump that a circus artist makes through a hoop which has been covered by paper. On one side, our side, is death. Ita's body lies limp, lifeless, but even as we look down into the grave and shield our faces, her spirit does a double somersault and jumps up, breathless and laughing on the grass beyond the hoop.

I think that's how it was for Jesus, that Friday afternoon, 2,000 years ago.

* *Lord Jesus Christ, risen from the dead, strengthen our faith in the face of suffering and death, so that we may bring your comfort to those who mourn.*

Day 56 *Isaiah 52.13 to 53.6*

The man of sorrows

I wonder when Jesus first realized that this prophecy referred to him, that he was destined to become the 'man of sorrows' who would be 'pierced through for our faults, crushed for our sins'. Did he know for a long time? Or did full realization come slowly, as his life unfolded? How very frightened he must have been. No wonder he needed those long nights in prayer, alone on the hillside, for he must have wept and argued with God many times before that last night in Gethsemane.

It seems to me important that we reflect upon Jesus' humanity in regards to his relationship with God, because we are so overawed by his divinity that sometimes we forget that he really was 'a man like us'. There is nothing in the scriptures to suggest that Jesus had full knowledge and understanding about what was going to happen to him – that knowledge would have grown slowly during the three years of his public life. I suspect that full realization of his messianic destiny came to him quite late and that this accounts for the dramatic change in his attitude once he had 'set his face towards Jerusalem'.

Did he confide in Mary Magdalene, I wonder? Was that why she made that amazing gesture with the ointment, anointing him in preparation for his death? How little we know about this man whose life and death give such meaning to our lives.

✱ ***Lord Jesus Christ, Man of Sorrows,***
you have known the agony of betrayal,
the pain of humiliation, and the fear of death.
Open our hearts to share your pain
and the pain of all who mourn.

Day 57 *Isaiah 53.7-12*

Jesus' descent into Hades

Where *was* Jesus on that terrible Sabbath when John was comforting Jesus' grieving mother, and Mary was waiting impatiently for the time when she would come with the precious spikenard to anoint his body. Did he really 'descend among the dead' as the Creed tells us? Did he go with his cross like a battering ram to break down the gates of Hades, to rescue our forefathers and the prophets?

I love the idea of the triumphant Jesus taking Hades by storm, the ancient image of what the Eastern Church calls the

Anastasis, the harrowing of Hell. Resurrection is not simply a rising from the dead but a glorious transformation of the Man of Sorrows into *Christus Vincit*, Christ the Conqueror, the glorious Messiah. We can imagine the scene, as if Christ has arrived at the gates of a Latin American prison camp, or a vast asylum for those with Alzheimer's disease: as the gates are broken down, there emerges a stream of radiant laughing people, released from the bonds of illness and death. *This* is how I understand resurrection, life after death.

✻ *Risen Lord, King of Kings, Gentle Messiah, we worship you.*
Break down the gates of every hell on earth,
so that the light of your truth
may penetrate our darkened world.

For personal reflection or group discussion

How can we make sense of the world's immense suffering in the light of the cross? What is the nature of our hope? And where do we discover joy?

ACTION

Spend some time this week with someone who is ill, severely handicapped, bereaved, or depressed.

CHRIST'S VICTORY

Notes based on the Revised Standard Version by

M Gnanavaram

M Gnanavaram is a priest from the Madurai-Ramnad Diocese of the Church of South India. He is now on the staff of the Tamilnadu Theological Seminary, Arasaradi, Madurai, South India, where he teaches New Testament.

The dramatic story of the resurrection of Jesus is attested to in the synoptic, Johannine and Pauline traditions of the New Testament. Every New Testament author presents this story in accordance with the life setting of his readers. Therefore in this week's meditations, we will attempt to relate the resurrection of Jesus to the everyday life of the people by

- considering what the text says;
- examining how it was relevant to those believers of the Old Testament and the first Christians;
- relating that message to our present context both at personal and social levels;
- ending with a short prayer for the day.

Dear God, our Father and Mother,
open our hearts to your word.

Day 58   Mark 16.1-8

(*cf also Matthew 28.1-7; Luke 24.1-12; John 20.1-10*)

Jesus rises from the dead

'Do not be amazed; . . . he is not here'

This is the important phrase to remember – Jesus has been raised. He could not be confined to the tomb. For the religious and political leaders, the tomb was a symbol of the defeat of Jesus' movement, and victory for them. Some knew and accepted that Jesus was innocent and righteous (Mark 15.39; Matthew 27.54; Luke 23.47; John 19.21; John 3.2; Acts 2.22). Religious and political powers of oppression joined together and tried to crush the movement of the Kingdom. It was the greatest injustice that the righteous Son of God was crucified (Acts 3.13-15). So Jesus' resurrection is a symbol of victory over injustice and oppression by both political and religious authorities.

What did it mean to the early disciples? Their fear was removed (note the angel's words, 'Do not be afraid' Mark 16.6). They were empowered to go and tell the good news. The disciples, who locked the doors of the house for the fear of the Jews (John 20.19), became courageous enough to stand outside and preach the good news (Acts 2.14ff).

What does this mean to you today? If you are afraid at a personal level, God says to you, 'Do not be afraid.' If you fear the unjust structures of this world, do not be dismayed. There is hope of victory over injustice and for a righteous world order in the resurrection of Jesus.

✸ *Lord, we thank you for giving us hope in hopelessness.*
We remember innocent people who are oppressed
by unjust political and religious authorities.
We pray for those places where religious fundamentalism
is used by political opportunists
to threaten the lives of innocent people.
Give us strength to work for their liberation.

Day 59   Mark 16.9-18
(cf also Matthew 28.16-20; Luke 24.13-35; John 20.24-31)

The power of the resurrection
'In my name they will cast out demons'

Jesus appears to his disciples and gives them authority over deadly things (Mark 16.18) such as demons, snakes, sickness and death-giving powers of destruction, and authority to preach the good news of liberation to the whole creation (Mk 16.15; Matthew 28.19-20; John 20.22-23). This is not the oppressive authority which operated in Jesus' crucifixion, but a liberating authority which transforms dehumanized people into human beings.

We read about the power of the resurrection in the life and ministry of the apostles and ministers in the Acts and the Epistles (Acts 2.4; 19.6; 28.5).

There are many situations where human beings suffer because of dehumanizing powers. They are political, socio-cultural, economic and religious in nature. Christ's resurrection gives us power and authority to work against these death-giving powers (Luke 4.18-19; John 20.21; Philippians 4.13).

✴ *Thank you Lord, that you give us power in our powerlessness.*
Give us wisdom to use your strength
to work for your glory in the service of your Kingdom,
for the freedom of your people
who suffer because of death-giving powers.

Day 60   1 Corinthians 15.1-12

The hope of future resurrection

'*How can some of you say there is no resurrection of the dead?*'

This chapter is the first surviving witness to the resurrection of Jesus outside the Gospel tradition. Paul brings out the relationship between Jesus' resurrection and the ultimate resurrection of believers. His argument for a bodily resurrection should be understood against the background of Gnosticism and the Sadducees who did not accept a bodily resurrection (Matthew 22.23).

For Paul, the body is as important as the soul. 'Body' symbolizes all matter, including experiences of history which relate to our whole life. Matter matters to God! Bodily resurrection is also the resurrection of the community, when God overcomes all enemies, death being the last enemy to be destroyed (1 Corinthians 15.24-26).

Our history of so many failures needs the hope of resurrection. God is concerned about our body, history and ecology. All the failures, irresponsibilities and incompleteness of our history will be set right.

✴ *Thank you, Lord, that all history is in your hands,*
and that you will complete our history
by the power of the resurrection of your Son Jesus Christ.
Help us to work with you
as you always work towards that completion.

                                                                                      John 5.17

Day 61 *Isaiah 42.10-16*

Resurrection and restoration

'I will turn the darkness before them into light'

In the 'Servant Song' of Isaiah 42, the author brings out a hope of restoration against the background of the sufferings of Israel in exile. God promises to bring them back to their land and give them joy and peace. It is God's messianic justice which will bring restoration (42.2-3). God will bring out prisoners from the dungeon, and release those who sit in darkness. He will turn the darkness before them into light (42.16). Like the resurrection of Jesus, these are impossible things for human beings, but not for God's mighty power.

The real experience of the Israelites was that God brought them from the land of Babylon. They praised God who restored their life in Israel. It was not a 'religious' experience but a historical experience.

This gives us enormous hope of restoration for our lives and encouragement to participate in the work of God for the restoration of justice to the marginalized and oppressed.

✸ *Dear God, our Father and Mother,*
we thank you that you are the God of compassion and justice;
for your promise to turn our darkness into light.
We pray for places where darkness prevails,
for political prisoners who are away from their homelands;
for countries where people experience instability and exploitation
because of the involvement of foreign powers.
We pray that you will bring justice and peace to them.

Day 62 *Romans 6.3-11*

Resurrection and new life
(cf Col 2.20-3.17)

'So we too might walk in newness of life ... dead to sin and alive to God'

The resurrection of Jesus gives us new life both at personal and social levels. But to experience this, we have to experience crucifixion. For Paul, this is to consider ourselves dead to sin: to crucify the death-giving aspects of life (Galatians 2.19). At a personal level, life comes through our negation of death-giving ways and through the power Christ gives. Many Christians stop at this level, but socially, life comes only through the voluntary suffering we accept for the sake of justice for the oppressed, exposing the power of evil and making people aware of it. This is what Jesus did on the cross (Colossians 2.14-15; John 12.31-32).

This was the experience of the Early Church. They negated the death-giving aspects of life and affirmed life-giving qualities: love, equality and sharing.

If we are willing to experience new life through Christ, we have to crucify the death-giving old order and affirm the ways of the life-giving new order.

✷ *Lord, we thank you for new life*
through the resurrection of your Son Jesus Christ.
Give us courage and wisdom
to work with you in giving life to others.

Day 63   Exodus 14.15 to 15.1

Resurrection and deliverance

'I will sing to the Lord, for he has triumphed gloriously'

Today's passage speaks about the great deliverance of the Israelites by the hand of God. What is the relationship between this incident and the resurrection of Jesus?

In the Old Testament, sea and deep waters symbolize danger and death. The Israelites are saved from the sea as well as from the oppressive hand of the Egyptians. The history of God's salvation is repeated in the glorious triumph of Jesus Christ over against death in his resurrection. Both events are miraculous triumphs of deliverance.

For the Israelites, God's hand meant deliverance from danger and death. In Jesus' resurrection, the early Christians experienced deliverance from death and so they were not afraid of dying for their faith.

Sometimes we find ourselves caught in a problem and do not see any way out. God in his power can open up a way for us. God wants us to work with him for the deliverance of others who are caught up in dangers of death. Christ gives us his power in our ministry of deliverance.

✷ *Lord, we thank you that you deliver us*
from all sorts of perils and dangers.
Thank you for saving us from death.
Help us to work for the deliverance of others
who are caught up in dangers of death.

Day 64 Acts 2.22-32

Resurrection and witness

'This Jesus God raised up, and of that all of us are witnesses'

In his first sermon on the day of Pentecost, Peter says that the experience of Pentecost itself is a witness to the resurrection of Jesus Christ. For this he brings scriptural evidence from the Old Testament.

The Early Church was a witness to the resurrection of our Lord Jesus (Acts 2.32; 3.15). How were they witnesses? By their resurrected lifestyle. It was a different lifestyle, rejecting conventions. It was a totally different model both in terms of religion, culture, society and economics (Acts 2.44-47; 4.32-37). In the same way, God expects us to witness to Jesus' resurrection through the challenging lifestyle of the church.

✱ *Thank you, Lord, for calling us to be your witnesses, for martyrs who gave their lives for rejecting unjust powers.*
Help us to witness to the resurrection of our Lord Jesus through our resurrected lives.

For personal reflection or group discussion

What are the death-giving aspects of your community or nation? What would 'resurrection' mean for your people? Where do you see signs of God's power already at work?

ACTION

How will you work with God to bring the different aspects of resurrection to your community and environment?

HYMNS OF PRAISE

Notes based on the Hebrew Bible by

Jonathan Magonet

Jonathan Magonet is a Rabbi who has specialized in the teaching of the Hebrew Bible. He is particularly interested in bringing readers back to the Hebrew text of the Bible so that forms of composition and the inner links between words and all their related nuances can be taken into account in trying to understand each individual passage.

The theme of 'praise' is difficult, especially when it comes from a book like the Psalms, so much of which was meant for public worship. While individual prayer is a private matter, public liturgies always have a 'political' dimension, because they also seek to define and educate the particular community. So the task of the interpreter is somehow to be true to the language and spirit of the Psalm as far as we can before remaking it in our own image.

For an introduction to the poetry of the Psalms and the different ways in which the same Psalm can be understood, the reader may like to consult Rabbi Magonet's *A Rabbi Reads the Psalms* (SCM Press 1994).

Day 65   Psalm 147

Exile and return

It rarely snows in Jerusalem, yet when it does the city is utterly transformed. Perhaps just such an experience inspired this Psalm, as well as some darker memories. The snow that blankets the city can suddenly melt and the water simply run away. Israel had once 'blanketed' the city with people, and then, also at God's command, been 'poured away' into exile. Now the writer, while celebrating their return, understands how their hold on the city depends upon obedience to the will and word of God.

For God's power is without limit: knowing each star of the sky by its name and summoning it to appear in its place; feeding every single creature on the earth and in the sky; watching over the destiny of every individual and of all nations, raising the lowly and humbling the wicked. It is not military power that determines the fate of nations but their fear and knowledge of God.

The awareness of this lies behind the Psalm, but now it is time to celebrate the restoration and to sing praises to God who punishes yet binds up wounds and heals the heart of those who have suffered.

✷ *Before Your cold who can stand?*
Sustain me with the warmth of Your word.

Day 66   *Psalm 19*

Inner and outer

Bible scholars have tended to see this Psalm as two parts that got stuck together: an original pagan hymn to the cosmos and a meditation on the inner life. It is easy to see why. The opening is a magnificent evocation of the sky at night and of the majestic path of the sun across the heavens. But the closing section speaks of our inner life, the forces acting within us, the drives that lead us into error, folly and arrogance. How are they related?

Between the two are six manifestations of God that together underpin the quality of human society. The first is *Torah*, often wrongly translated as 'law'. Rather it means 'teaching', 'direction', the 'way'. In the Hebrew, the six sentences, with their exact parallel structure, are like the rungs of a ladder, uniting the outer and inner worlds, holding together the universe and the individual human soul.

What is our personal ladder that links our inner and outer selves? Our Psalm itself offers no answer but ends with a prayer and a plea for personal integrity.

✷ *May the words that actually come to my lips*
and the inner thought in my heart
together be acceptable to You, my God.

Day 67 *Psalm 135*

The use and abuse of tradition

This Psalm feels like a sampler – 'the best of the Temple Psalms'! With minor variations, you will find these parallels:

verse 1 = Psalm 113.1;
verse 2 = Psalm 134.1;
verse 6 = Psalm 115.3;
verses 15-18 = Psalm 115.4-8;
verses 19-20 = Psalm 115.9-11 and Psalm 118.2-4.

It also quotes variations on other Bible verses:

verse 4 = Deuteronomy 7.6;
verse 7 = Jeremiah 10.13;
verse 9 = Exodus 7.3;
verse 13 = Exodus 3.15;
verse 14 = Deuteronomy 32.36.

God is the ruler of nature (verses 6-7) and of human history (verses 8-12), supreme above all the other imagined gods of the nations (verses 5 and 15-18), and therefore free to choose Israel as God's special people (verses 4, 12 and 14). The traditional quotations reinforce these themes and may be intended to reassure a nation whose self-confidence has been shaken. God is still our God; the ancient covenant is still binding; history is still moving towards the acceptance of God by the nations of the world.

So is the Psalm simply a case of the triumphalism that so often emerges in times of religious doubt? At the heart is still a call for self-criticism and repentance: 'God will judge His people!'

✳ *May I never hide behind my tradition
from the task I must face today.*

Day 68 *Psalm 30*

When our world falls apart

The Temple contained 'off the peg' Psalms. Someone who went through a difficult experience might vow to bring an offering to God if saved. Now, standing before the community to offer thanks, the person would select a Psalm that most fitted the danger that had overcome him or her.

So what has this writer gone through – a severe illness, a bereavement, a life-threatening event, a fall from office or power? Something shattered the Psalmist's customary feeling of being 'at home' in the world. 'I said in my "safety", "security", I shall never slip!' But when the world fell apart, those certainties went, and only emptiness and terror remained.

Anyone who has seen the bottom drop out of their world can recognize this experience: a love gone sour, a betrayal by someone we trusted, a medical diagnosis that transforms our life. For some, turning to God might seem normal; others may feel it is like cheating, to pray just because 'the chips are down'. The Psalmist seems to know all these feelings, and tells us they are all legitimate, for God is waiting to be found.

✷ *In my joy,*
let me not forget the troubles that once beset me;
in my trouble, give me the help I need.

Day 69 *Psalm 40*

The enemy within

A highly individual personality emerges in this Psalm, especially if we notice how certain words are used both of God and the Psalmist (though these are not obvious in all translations):

- God's deeds are '*more* than can be *numbered*' (verse 5) – I experience evils beyond *numbering* ... *more* than the hairs of my head (verse 12);
- You do not *desire* sacrifices (verse 6) – I *desire* to do Your will (verse 8);
- I have not *restrained* my lips (verse 9) – do not *restrain* Your mercy from me (verse 11);
- God has *thoughts* for 'us' (verse 5) – have *thoughts* for me! (verse 17)

It is a kind of negotiation. Knowing God's power and our powerlessness, all we can do is cajole, or barter, or plead. We struggle to hold on to our ego, our identity, our self-respect, knowing that we have to let them go. 'I desire to do Your will'. But knowing this and doing it are not the same.

The 'enemies' seem to be internal here rather than external – our own taunting voices, the sins that keep us from God. The 'quaking pit' is still there, and God has to be found again and again.

✷ *You are my help and my deliverer; do not tarry, my God!*

Day 70   Psalm 9
The passing of earthly powers

This Psalm seems to speak of certainties – that God's justice will prevail; that those who set out to conquer others will in the end be defeated; that their very arrogance will trap them – 'let the nations know they are but men'.

But is it composed out of personal experience of God's victory, or does it simply express a hope? The opening is a hymn of gratitude for God's triumph over enemies, whose very conquests will be forgotten. But in verse 13* comes the personal plea for rescue from 'the hands of those who hate me'. Is this quoting the plea of the 'humble' mentioned in verse 12*? or is it the actual author, having asserted confidence in God's power, finally asking for help?

(* These verses are numbered differently in the Hebrew Bible in which the title counts as verse 1).

The Psalm is also a meditation on Genesis 9.5 – 'God seeks out' the shedder of blood (the common translation '*avenges blood*' in verse 12* is misleading). It reflects a Rabbinic teaching: that God is always on the side of the victim, and the painful reality that once violence begins it is not easily stopped. So the Psalmist's prayer can be ours:

✱ *Arise, O Lord, do not let man prevail –*
   let the nations know they are but men!

Day 71   Psalm 145
The missing letter

This Psalm is an alphabetical acrostic in the Hebrew. And it has a very formal structure: the three central verses, 11-13, acclaim God as King; the previous verses describe how creation praises God, and the following ones highlight the generosity with which God sustains creation.

Such formality suggests some kind of religious complacency – everything is all right in a world ruled by God. But sometimes formality is a defence against a world where there is actually very little certainty and no room for complacency. Asserting God's rule may be a defence against the anarchy without and our fear of dissolution within.

God provides enough for all but there is one crucial element missing from the picture. 'You open Your hand and satisfy all the living with their needs' – but only if we provide the human hands to ensure this.

One letter is missing from the alphabetic acrostic – perhaps out of ancient fears of perfect formality. But this leaves room for our own contribution, the letter we have to provide. Without it the promise of the psalm, the maintenance of the world under God, would simply fall apart.

✷ *Open our hands,*
so we can satisfy the needs of the world.

For personal reflection or group discussion

1. How far is my prayer life 'my own' private affair, and how far is it affected by the formal liturgies of my community?

2. How much of my liturgy can I take at face value and how much do I have to 'interpret' for myself?

3. If there is a conflict between what my formal prayers say and what I believe or feel, where do I find the personal strength or authority to find my own way?

4. If my liturgy is intended in part to colour my way of thinking, and help create a 'community' of shared values, what responsibility should I take in its creation and development?

5. If I accept its values and teachings, how far do they actually affect the way I live my life?

ACTION

When reciting the phrase, 'You open Your hands and satisfy the need of every living thing' (Psalm 145.16), there is a Jewish tradition of opening up our hands, palms outwards, to symbolize God's actions in feeding the world. Food is available for all God's creatures, but we have to be the distribution network – 'God's hands'. Some congregations have opened up their building to provide 'hospitality luncheons' once a week for the local unemployed and street people, with a hot meal, bathroom facilities and clothes, friendship and care. This programme can be undertaken by any community that is willing to provide the 'missing letter' in Psalm 145 and make our own small contribution to feeding the world.

BE PREPARED FOR OPPOSITION

Notes based on the Good News Bible by

Magali do Nascimento Cunha

Magali do Nascimento Cunha is a young, lay journalist who works for an ecumenical organization in Brazil: Koinonia – Ecumenical Presence and Service. She is involved as a volunteer in projects of Christian Education for poor communities in Baixada Fluminense (on the outskirts of Rio de Janeiro).

'To live is not easy,' is a saying heard from birth by most people in Brazil. As life is not easy, it means that it is full of adversities and challenges, and we need to be prepared for them and get ready to overcome them.

Even God, who gave people freedom to decide the way to follow, had to face opposition and adversities and has taught us how to cope with and overcome them. Courage and strength to continue life's journey come from the Lord. Let us learn from him!

Day 72 *Matthew 13.53-58*

Facing and practising rejection

It isn't easy to be a (true) prophet! Reading the prophetic testimonies of the Bible, we learn that a prophet was destined to face opposition. The explanation is not difficult: sin is present in human nature, impelling people and groups to oppress each other. So it is not easy to shout against it and show that God's will is different.

One sin is prejudice, which Jesus encountered many times in his journey. 'How could a carpenter's son have such wisdom?' 'Can anything good come from Nazareth?' (John 1.46). For the narrow minds of traditional Israelite society the role of prophet implied status. Of course, those 'false prophets' who worked to sustain tradition and oppression had status ... Jesus was rejected. Being poor, he could never be a prophet!. Think about

Jesus' experience at his home town (Luke 4.16-30). Has your authority been questioned when you thought you were doing right, or working for the benefit of others?

Have you been prejudiced at any time? Have you rejected the challenge of another person as inferior? How can we be true prophets today and defend God's will?

✳ *Dear Lord,*
 Help me to understand and accept your will.
 Help me to accept and learn from the messages
 that come through simple people. Amen.

Day 73   Isaiah 59.12-20

'Rowing against the tide'

The years 1964 to 1978 are known in Brazil as 'the age of the darkness'. It was the time when the military dictatorship imprisoned, tortured and killed thousands of people who opposed the regime and fought for democracy. It is a long and sad story of many young people, workers, students, teachers, poor and rich, men and women, who knew the risks but offered their lives for what they believed: freedom and justice for all Brazilians.

They were 'rowing against the tide'; they were opposers of an oppressive system. Perhaps many of them did not know, but they were prophets and martyrs who were – in holy action – defending the will of God.

We learn about that through Isaiah. 'The Lord is displeased that there is no justice ... he will use his own power ... he will wear justice like a coat of armour, he will come like a rushing river, like a strong wind ...' (verses 15-19). Yes. The Lord is ready to oppose injustice and oppression. He gives us strength even if we are 'rowing against the tide'. It is a fight to defend God's will, reinforced with mercy and love. In ordinary situations of life or in something bigger in community or society, let's clothe ourselves with justice, mercy and love.

✳ *Our God, thank you for giving us strength*
 and courage to defend your will.
 Do not let us to be afraid of serving you.
 In Jesus' name. Amen

Day 74   *Amos 7.10-17*

The wind blows wherever it wishes

Like Jesus, Amos faced prejudice. How could a herdsman come and preach against the king? There was prejudice in that question but there was something more. Kings' actions were sustained by prophets and priests; how could they be contested? The people believed they spoke in the name of God; how could Amos come in the name of the same God and cause agitation? For 'God's people' nothing appeared to be wrong. The structure was there, firm, stable, secure. How could anyone shake it?

The Spirit of the Lord could! God's action through Amos was there to show that God is not imprisoned within structures which can prevent the realization of God's will for their own benefit. The Holy Spirit, like a wind, blows and shakes, changes, and provokes movements that impel simple people like Amos to leave everything behind and preach, defending human rights, against all oppression. Amos was rejected and humiliated, but the Spirit who moved him to act gave him power to face opposition.

How important it is to learn from this experience! Our churches and religious groups need to reflect how pernicious structures can be, if they are not ready to serve. For service is the reason for their existence. We need to reflect how important it is to be ready to move with the wind and leave behind all security and stability. We will then be working for the right of life, the most precious gift we have from God.

✶ *Come Holy Spirit,*
prepare us to change everything that imprisons
the life that comes from you. Amen

Day 75   *Jeremiah 1.4-19*

Do not be afraid

It isn't easy to be a prophet! Jeremiah knew it well, even being so young. He also knew how to listen to the Lord's voice and that happened very early in his life. He felt fear, a very human feeling.

Jeremiah's experience shows to us how the Lord's mission is for all. Old and young, rich or poor, all of us are called to take part. Jeremiah has inspired young people in our churches in Brazil to find ways to serve the Lord. His voice comes to them and to all of us today: 'Do not say you are too young, but go to the people I send you to ...'

When we decide to serve the Lord, adversities and difficulties can come but as he promised to Jeremiah, 'Do not be afraid. I will be with you.' A Latin American song sung at youth gatherings expresses the challenge:

'I need to shout, I need to risk
Woe is me if I do not do it!
How can I escape from you?
How can I silence
if your voice burns inside me?'

✷ *Our God, forgive our fear and incapacity to overcome it.*
We are nothing without you.
Touch our lips and speak through us
to those who need to listen to your voice. Amen

Day 76   *Isaiah 49.6-7*

Hope is alive

For more than twenty years, the Bible has been rediscovered in Latin America by many Christian communities. Theologians have called this process 'Biblical Spring'. The beauty of this experience is to link the Bible story to our own story today, to discover what we have in common and how we can learn from the experience of God's people in the past.

The fact that the Hebrew people suffered – the humiliation of slavery, oppression by their own kings, exile and loss of dignity – identifies with the sufferings of our people today. There is the humiliation, like slavery, of working for low salaries, of being oppressed by self-interested governors, of losing citizenship and dignity for the sake of big business ...

Going deeper, what is great is to discover that there is a God, who was there in the past and is here in our present. The Lord God is the bearer of all hope that humiliation and suffering will have an end. That is the reason for God being hated and opposed by the nations (verse 7). However, God is greater than all opposers and is faithful. He fulfils his promises to restore the greatness of the people and bring them to life.

God's promises are alive today. We need to listen to them and become as servants, a light to the world, bringing hope to all who need it to survive. The Bible is our instrument for doing that. How can we bring it to life?

✱ *Lord, thank you for your Word through the Bible.*
I praise you for your faithfulness and greatness.
Praise be to you this day!

Day 77   *Psalm 17*
Opposing and defeating enemies

'Come Lord, oppose my enemies and defeat them!' How can we pray today, using the words of the psalmist? What are the meanings of this prayer for us? Who are our enemies today?

Sometimes Christians spiritualize this reflection, identifying 'the enemy' as the Devil. By exorcizing the Devil from our lives, our problems would be solved. Isn't that an easy solution? Maybe. But evil is also present in our world to oppose God's justice and peace. What or who is the Devil?

The enemy, most times, is ourselves. Yes! How many times do we opt for attitudes that cause bad consequences, just by using the freedom God gives us? When we fall into temptation sometimes we fall by our own nature and personality which become our enemies. When Jesus was tempted in the desert, the Devil offered him those things that human nature always fights for: power, wealth, political domination. Aren't they? Jesus' faithfulness to the Kingdom's values is a great lesson to us. Sin is more than the immorality to which it is reduced by many Christian groups. It is part of human nature – the enemy within us which is ready to act if we permit it.

If we accept the presence of God in our lives and decide to live for his Kingdom, sin will still be present, as we are human, but it will be a defeated enemy and we will really be new creatures.

✱ *Come, dear Lord, to my life*
and your presence will fill me with joy.

Day 78   *Romans 16.25-27*
The Lord supports and liberates

Many temptations and trials come to us that make us weaker and lose our faith. Paul says that we can praise the Lord because he is able to make us stand firm according to the good news of Jesus Christ and according to God's promises through the prophets.

So, God can make our faith firm, both making us grow in the knowledge of the truth and helping us to avoid mistakes that break us. That is a great teaching from Paul: if we want to grow in faith we need to learn about the truth through the writings of the prophets.

The knowledge of the Word of God, the testimonies that come from Jesus, from the prophets, and from all those anonymous people who had an experience with God, is a source of strength to us who face all sorts of adversities in our world. What testing times have we faced? In our family ... in our work ... in our community ... in our church ...? Remember again the temptations Jesus faced in the desert. Think again about the values of the Kingdom of God, about Jesus' teachings.

Thanks be to God for his action among us and his support. But let's be ready to act and overcome the adversities and not accept them easily. Be firm and trust the Lord!

✴ *Glory be to you, our Lord, for your mercy and support.*
Do not lead us into temptation
but deliver us from evil. Amen

For personal reflection or group discussion

1. Have you felt called to do something in the name of God? Have you felt afraid or ashamed of acting in God's name? What were the difficulties? Think about the testimonies of Amos and Jeremiah. What can you learn from them and apply to your own experience?

2. What temptations come to you? Can you identify them easily? Compare them with the temptations Jesus faced. What can you learn from Jesus' experience and apply to your life?

ACTION

Identify in your daily life, in family, work or community, situations that require your action as a prophet, both speaking or acting. Ask for God's help, and struggle to do the will of God.

THE SPIRIT SHARES OUR STRUGGLE

Reflections based on the New Revised Standard Version by

Jane Ella P Montenegro

Jane Montenegro, a Filipino, was gripped by Christ's liberating gospel in the Martial Law period. She moved into Christian Education within and outside the Church, working in both urban and rural areas. Today she facilitates workshops on liturgical renewal, children's work, and the empowerment of women. She is presently pastor of a mountain church while studying Asian feminist theology.

To commit oneself to the work of Jesus Christ for truth, justice and peace is to plunge into the darkness of life. It means being with the fearful, the ignorant, the anguished, the lost – victims of socio-economic, cultural, political exploitation. Sharing hardship means taking risks, extending into more complicated struggles, linking creatively with varied structures, with a deeper thirst for inner light.

Inspired by the Spirit of God, we work with those who share this passion for 'peace on earth, good will toward all humankind and creation'.

Day 79   *John 15.18-27*

Sharing the burden of being hated

As a child, I believed that one must be submissive, at peace with everyone at home, school, church, among neighbours – everywhere. But later experience taught me otherwise.

At 16, a trumped-up letter destroyed my father's career, because he counselled against marital infidelity. Some years later, while in government service, our Faculty Club complained about salary deductions without prior consultation, and the Church has questioned other irregularities. In these painful events, interpersonal relationships were blocked, school and church authorities preached against each other, intrigues ran high and trust and friendships were broken. Certainly Jesus' admonition becomes an assuring reality. 'I have chosen you out of the world – therefore the world hates you.'

Will you follow the way of Jesus: being maligned, misunderstood and isolated? Will you lighten your anguish and burdens and let them be shared with others who seek truth and peace? Then together, we can grow in faith, by our shared struggle and hardships for Christ's sake.

✳ *O Spirit of Christ, come.*
Blaze this darkness among us with your truth.
O Spirit of Peace, come.
Heal our woundedness together. Amen

Day 80   *Matthew 10.16-23*

Living with death

Jesus tells his disciples how to live with death: to be wise and innocent among their persecutors, to be still and alert to what the Spirit wants them to say to the powers-that-be. They would be hated for proclaiming his name. They would run for their lives, escaping – if possible – premature death.

Almost 2,000 years later, these texts come alive to a mountain church in Mindanao. During the 1980s and until the early 1990s, this area of the Philippines was notorious as the 'killing fields' of peasants and other suspected rebels of the government of President Marcos. Soldiers and a para-military unit controlled this zone. Innocent farmers were beaten up or hacked to death while the perpetrators went free.

A community of faith persevered, encouraging one another in birthday serenades, Sunday School and worship, family rituals and thanksgiving celebrations. They learnt endurance from each other and shared their hardship in prayer. Their faith in Christ grew – despite the complex political ideologies and the preservation of national security.

✳ *O Spirit of Christ,*
may this shared experience of persecution
become my lesson of renewal
and commitment towards peace. Amen

Day 81 *Acts 4.1-22*

The Spirit shares the hardship of the helpless

It is an old, powerful story, culturally and religiously rooted. It shaped the very core of their beings. It had been shared from clan to clan, generation to generation. It is the story of shared hardship among the weak and how the strong are toppled by God's mighty acts.

So it was with Moses and Pharaoh, David and Goliath, Esther and the King, and now Peter and John with the religious aristocracy. Neither imprisonment nor a ban on teaching about Jesus could stop them.

Contemporary events confirm for us the unpredictable movement of the Holy Spirit. The end of the Philippine Martial Law Regime in 1986 was a miracle of prayers, bread, flowers and songs surrounding government soldiers and tanks of war. Mandela's election to the Presidency of South Africa in 1994 toppled decades of bitter suffering under apartheid. This is the essence of the Kingdom. God shares the hardships of the weak and helpless and grants them victory in the end.

✷ *O empowering Spirit, let me be full of faith in you,*
that in my weakness I may share
in turning the world upside down for others' sake. Amen

Day 82 *Acts 5.17-32*

Share to dare

The bonding of the apostles made them strong enough to dare to confront the Temple hierarchy. Most probably, they shared strategies and planned how to proceed with the proclamation of God's saving acts. Then, miracle of miracles ... ! More boldly and joyfully than ever they shared together, daring their opposers with the message of the Holy Spirit. Faced by the most powerful men in the land, they stood firm in their faith conviction.

Centuries later, this bold encounter with religious authorities has been shared by many women reformers and martyrs, as well as men, influencing them to act towards change, like Joan of Arc, condemned as a heretic and burnt at the stake. Melchora Aquino and Gabriela Silang became Filipino martyrs during the Spanish regime, and thousands more unnamed women and men have been persecuted, but the daring for the gospel's sharing has not been stopped.

The natural world shares our groans (page 83)
Woodcut by Boy Dominguez, the Philippines

✷ *O Spirit of power, help us to share and dare
for the transformation of Church and society today.
In Jesus' name. Amen*

Day 83   Romans 8.18-25
The natural world shares our groans

I learnt to swim in a river teeming with small fish. The forest that I loved had giant trees with eagles, hornbills, orioles, colourful butterflies and insects with fascinating shapes. We ate upland rice that was black, pink, red or creamy white. Each variety smelt sweet and tasted deliciously different from the other. I would sing heartily, '... the valleys stand so thick with corn ...' My feelings were deep. I was very aware of my soul. God was everywhere!

Today, the river is dry. It is filled with junk and garbage. The giant trees have long been sold by a logging company to countries that do not cut down trees. There are no more eagles, nor hornbills that caw. Our variety of rice is decided by the International Research Rice Institute. How can I sing when the valleys are brown and the ears of corn have become like the fist of a child?

I feel an aching emptiness – a sense of loss. Will the deep feelings, a sense of connectedness to the earth ever return? Will learning again from indigenous old women be part of the answer and a sign of hope?

✷ *O Creator God, let me be courageous to redeem
one groaning piece of the earth as my offering to you!*

Day 84   Romans 8.26-27
The Spirit shares our weakness

Depay was heavy with child – her tenth when I met her. Pale and thin, she was stretching her crumpled skirt repeatedly, letting her women neighbours speak up for her. Two weeks ago, she and her husband Pedro had just sold their corn products and were going back to the farm when a man accosted them on the road, demanding their corn sale at knife-point. Depay pleaded for mercy. She was pushed violently aside. It happened so quickly. Pedro bled to death on the road. No one was willing to testify as witness. The roadside houses were closed. But in whispers, the village women identified the killer as a notorious military man who was absent without leave from his assignment. Yes, we can make the report for Depay to sign, but the police will only receive it. The village councillors cannot do much either. There is no justice.

✴ *O grieving Spirit of God, help us to discern
that you are here in our suffering and powerlessness.
And teach us how to pray – in Jesus' name. Amen*

Day 85   Revelation 1.9-20
Sharing a vision of Christ

In Revelation, John transports us to his divine experience. He describes Christ vividly in minute detail: the colours, figures, numbers, metals, elements and vestments. One can smell and feel the flame of fire from Christ's eyes and the blazing rays from his face. His voice is multi-toned. Did it sound like a brook, ripples on a stream, a waterfall, the ebb tide on the shore, an undersea current, or the crest of ocean waves? Ah, what magical tones!

Hundreds more have had mystical experiences which they alone could fathom. What matters most is that after a spiritual revelation, we are converted by the Spirit – committed to bring wholeness to the world.

✴ *O Divine Spirit, forbid it not
that I should receive your revelation. Amen*

For personal reflection or group discussion

What injustices are suffered in your country? To what extent have you shared them, and how costly has that been? When has the presence of Christ been most real?

ACTION

Find out more about the issues that affect the Philippines. Pray for Christians who witness in this situation.

If you would like to continue reading the Bible with IBRA, don't forget to fill in and send off the form on page 120.

RESPONDING TO BLINDNESS

Notes based on the New Revised Standard Version by

Jane Wallman

Jane Wallman, an Anglican priest in Woodbridge (UK), is a part-time research fellow at the University of Birmingham developing an understanding of Christian thought from the perspective of disabled people. Born visually impaired, Jane uses a guide dog.

The next time you find yourself in a busy place, pause for a moment and shut your eyes. In a few seconds, a sense of disorientation compels you to open your eyes and reassert your independence. The world of a visually-impaired person is small. It stretches as far as a cane will reach or a guide dog will lead. It contains much that is unidentifiable, frightening and inconclusive.

John Hull in *Touching the Rock* writes frankly about the difference losing his sight made to him as a committed Christian. Helen Keller's philosophy of life summed up in Anna Sullivan's biography of this deaf-blind woman, perhaps captures best the essence of a life without visual images: 'Life is a daring adventure or it is nothing at all.'

Day 86   *John 9.1-12*

How were your eyes opened?

The blind man, at his regular spot, waited for donations. A familiar figure, caught-up in his interior world, non-productive in society's eyes, known for his disability and not for who he was – the story he had to tell.

Jesus was quick to dismiss any connection between sinfulness and disability. He stressed that the man had been born as God intended him to be so that God's own power might be displayed. The man received from Christ the gift of sight. He did not seek the gift, but he did recognize the uniqueness of the giver and accepted his part in enabling Christ to fulfil his destiny as Messiah. He defended Jesus to those who were curious. Once blind, he was now a physical manifestation of the Light of the World illuminating and energizing every aspect of life. He seized, with all his heart and mind, new life with God.

✳ *God of darkness and light,*
touch me gently, speak to me softly, and guide me
on the path towards your healing and love. Amen

Day 87   *John 9.13-34*
Let him speak for himself

The man's change of circumstance defied conventional teaching. It spoke of power, mystery and energy. The Pharisees failed to see the truth. As the man told his story with conviction and simplicity – so the Pharisees' shallowness was exposed.

The man who was identified by what he lacked, was suddenly known by all he had gained. He faced the Pharisees and explained the nature of Jesus as he then understood it – Jesus was a healer working through God's power and blessing. Change is painful. The Pharisees returned to their trusted Law. The man, healed, faced disbelief in others, yet still chose to embrace new life.

Change is about perceiving an opportunity and daring to risk engaging with the new and different; turning from the darkness to the light.

✳ *God of love,*
let my lips speak of all you have done for me.
Let my voice sing your praise.
Let my heart yearn to be what you would have me be
and let my mind long to pray. Amen

Day 88   *John 9.35-41*
Jesus found him

The blind man never once sought Jesus. Thrown out by the Pharisees, he was told in no uncertain terms that either he or his parents had sinned. The man could not fail to be hurt and dejected as those in authority reduced his dignity and worth once again. An old, familiar pattern within him – feeling set apart and seen as different – returned. Although physically healed, he was still regarded as an outcast. The thing he had most wanted brought him pain as well as joy.

Jesus sought him out. Jesus recognized his need before he saw it in himself. Jesus drew the man on in his understanding. The man recognized the invitation and fell on his knees: 'Lord, I believe.'

✷ *Light of the world,*
you know our needs before we cry to you.
You know our hopes before we dare to dream them.
Find us and fill us with your light and love.

Day 89   Mark 4.10-12
Seeing is believing
My father was a professional magician. He did impossible tricks with playing cards, coins, and all sorts of things. He often said: 'The quickness of the hand deceives the eye.' The harder you look to see how a trick is done, the less likely you are to discover! We all know that awful feeling when we lose something important. I've learnt, as a visually-impaired person, that searching is often frustrating, so I sit down and work out a timetable: when did I last have it? What happened next and so on. In the quietness of reflecting, the object is usually found.

The blessing of spiritual insight is a gift that God gives to those who are devoted followers. On our faith pilgrimage it is all too easy to become caught up in the searching for greater vision and fail to see the bountiful joys our limited 'vision' is already showing us.

✷ *O Thou who hast given me eyes*
to see the light that fills my room,
give me the inward vision to behold thee in this place.
    C Devanesen, India – Morning Noon and Night (CMS)

Day 90   Revelation 3.14-22
What are you looking for?
I have yet to meet a blind person who does not long to see. Blindness makes you vulnerable. You are public property. You have little privacy. You are a pull on the resources, an object of concern and care. You are the sum total of what others suspect you cannot do.

Laodicea was charged with being 'blind and naked', vulnerable in the midst of greater strength – the power of God. 'Blindness' here is used in an insulting way; it is not a means of greater stillness and insight, but the inability of a community to see the error of their ways. Here, the writer assumes that physical sightlessness equates with an inability to see truth – stumbling in the path of God. The writer's image is not a helpful one. In reality, if you don't know where you're going, a blind person is one of the safest people to guide you: s/he knows every centimetre of the route!

The charge against Laodicea and each one of us is that we allow pride to get in the way of our love of Christ and action in his name.

✱ *The things, good Lord, that we pray for, give us grace to labour for.*

St Thomas More (1478-1535)

Day 91   2 Kings 6.8-17
Standing in the need of prayer

Fear causes blind spots in all of us. Elisha's servant faced his own fear – that he might be captured by the enemy. He returned panic-stricken to his master. It was Elisha's prayer that the servant would see things in perspective that turned the story round.

The able-bodied often pray for the less able. In this story the power of intercession is in mutuality, recognizing the often hidden prayers of other people and folding them into our own prayers for ourselves. Elisha's prayer that his servant's eyes would be opened to see the massive power and strength of God's own army was also a cry that Elisha would himself trust the 'chariots of fire' and not visualize a city in destruction.

Look not only for support from those who seem stronger and better, but also to those who seem weaker and more vulnerable.

✱ *Open my eyes God,
to see the potential and not the problem,
to spot the opportunity and not halt at the obstacle,
to gaze on difference and make it my own. Amen*

Day 92   Ephesians 5.6-14
Life in Christ

Light and dark are powerful images of good and evil: life with Christ and life outside the community of the faithful.

For a person who cannot see well, the contrast and definition of light can be distorted. Light can be diffused or a pinprick of perception in an otherwise dark panorama. Light can actually blind rather than help to locate where a person is. Light is most effective as a metaphor for illumination; for focusing the truths that no one can actually see; a metaphor for viewing the universe; a vocabulary for framing and responding to the question of all time: why?

The light for all Christians is the light of firsthand encounter with Christ. We are encouraged to be comfortable with our experience, to be courageous in sharing, to delight in life and so point others to the power of God's interaction with creation.

✷ *May the light of God dance in my heart,*
the warmth of God sparkle in my eyes
and fall from my lips,
the energy of God make me open to wisdom and love.

For personal reflection or group discussion
God promises that he will bring good news to the poor, free the oppressed and restore sight to the blind (Luke 4.18). How can I award more dignity and mutuality to those who are different from myself? To those who frighten me or make me feel uncomfortable?

ACTION
Make an effort to talk to people with disabilities. Get to know each disabled person as an individual. Try not to assume too much or ask too many personal questions. When I am asked, 'Why are you blind?' after three minutes acquaintance, I often feel like asking the enquirer something equally personal in retaliation! Don't be put off by your own awkwardness or uncertainty. People with disabilities are used to dealing with non-disabled peoples' anxieties. Award the person with disabilities the same level of dignity, independence and courtesy you would give to your greatest friends. Allow them to tell their story and inform you. Enjoy sharing your true self with them.

PEOPLE OF GOD

Notes based on the Revised English Bible by

Bernard Thorogood

After serving 18 years in the Pacific islands with the London Missionary Society, Bernard Thorogood became General Secretary of the Society, which in 1977 was re-formed as the Council for World Mission. From 1980 to 1992, he was General Secretary of the United Reformed Church in Britain. He is now a minister of the Uniting Church of Australia.

All people on earth are people of God, for all are within God's purpose and care. So it may seem presumptuous to single out particular people and claim for them a special relationship with God – even more so when we apply that to ourselves.

Yet God does call people to the adventure of faith, does awaken the conscience, does give signs of healing power. God came at one point in history to a place in the person of Jesus, who called people to be with him. What then can it mean to be people of God in a world that is God's?

Day 93   Deuteronomy 7.6-11

How odd of God to choose the Jews

Yes, it was surprising and the ancient writers realized this. The earth was filled with tribes, so why should this one be selected? It was certainly not because of its power (verse 7), nor was it to become the most powerful. Always an insignificant nation caught between empires, it could only be special for its language, its way of life and its faith.

What can we understand by God's choice? God loves the world and makes the sun to shine and the rain to fall on the just and the unjust. 'To him, nations are but drops in a bucket . . . coasts and islands weigh as light as specks of dust!' (Isaiah 40.15). God is not like a child playing with toys and picking out his favourite.

But God reveals himself. 'He spoke in many and varied ways through the prophets' (Hebrews 1.1) and so became known to particular people at points of human history. Most clearly, most consistently, God became known to this people, a voice in Abraham's heart, a clear call to Moses and so through the centuries. They were chosen to respond, and as they received more light, so they had greater tasks.

✶ *We pray for the Jewish people,*
thanking God for their tradition of worship and prayer
into which Jesus was born,
and seeking for them continued light from God
and peace with their neighbours.

Day 94 Exodus 19.1-13

God and Israel – Covenant

The exodus from Egypt was an act of liberation. Israel was set free to become a nation. But what kind of nation would it be? Corrupt and feeble? Dependent and beggarly? Every liberation poses the same question which is answered as the life of the people unfolds.

At this point in the book of Exodus, we come to the crisis when the history of Israel depends on their hearing the claim of God and on their response to him. The call is to accept a binding relationship between God and the people (verse 5). At the beginning of Exodus, we read that God 'called to mind his covenant with Abraham, Isaac and Jacob; he observed the plight of Israel and took heed of it' (Exodus 2.24). Now the covenant is to be affirmed with the whole nation and the heart of it is that Israel will be God-like; as God is holy, so they are called to be (verse 6).

People do take on the quality of the gods they perceive and worship. If we think of God as distant and unconcerned for human life, then we are likely to have little compassion. But for us the character of God is shown in the life of Jesus Christ. So we know more surely what the word 'holy' means and therefore the quality of God's servant people.

✶ *Covenant God. You are our God,*
giving us new life and hope by your Spirit.
May we never forget you, deny you, dishonour you.
This day and every day we are yours.

Day 95   *Exodus 19.14-25*

God and Israel – Thunder

There are scholars who trace all the wonderful signs at Sinai to volcanic activity. It may have been so. The cloud and fire and thunder, the danger of approaching the summit all suggest this. But the key thought here is not how such things happened. It is how they became a revealing of the wonder of God.

We are taken back to an early stage of the human story. God was powerful – storms and rocks were split at his command. God was terrible – plagues flowed from his anger. God was supreme – no one could escape his judgment. To approach God, to stand in God's presence, was a fearful thing. Only Moses could go near; all the others had to keep their distance.

The risen Christ stood among his disciples. Come close, he said to Thomas, touch these scarred hands. Come, lads, let us have breakfast. I call you my friends.

We are filled with awe that the God who spoke at Sinai comes to share our life and our death, Emmanuel, God with us.

✱ *Not far beyond the sea, nor high*
  Above the heavens, but very nigh
    Thy voice, O God, is heard.
  For each new step of faith we take
  Thou hast more truth and light to break
    Forth from thy holy word.   *G B Caird*

Day 96   *Exodus 20.1-17*

God and Israel – Law

If, as Paul writes in Galatians, the Law was like a schoolmaster, then here is the supreme tutor, not just for the Israelites, but for the beginnings of human society.

The first three commands have to do with worship. That is where morality begins, lifting our eyes from the idols that we make to the Lord who creates us. Verse 7 reminds us that the name of God was precious and powerful, not to be misused. 'Hallowed be Thy name,' we pray, and it is the work of the Holy Spirit to cry the new name, 'Abba, Father' (Romans 8.15).

Verses 8 to 11 give stringent rules for a rest day and these were interpreted with ever-stricter details through the centuries. Jesus reminds his followers that the Sabbath is for their good, for life and health, not an imprisonment (Mark 2.27). Do the Sabbath rules apply to Sunday?

The other commands teach us how to live at peace in human community and in our families. They remain the basic laws for all, a minimum requirement. In Matthew 5 Jesus calls us to set even higher standards, for the desires of our hearts are the roots of action.

✷ *We cannot doubt your law of life and justice, Lord,*
  but we are a disobedient people.
  We seek forgiveness in Christ and life in the Spirit.

Day 97   *Deuteronomy 11.8-17*

God and Israel – Promise

The attachment of a nation to its land is very deep. Often it is the land which defines a nation, so that arguments about boundary lines become violent struggles. After the exodus, the Israelites were wanderers seeking a land where they could make a permanent home. In this passage, they are promised a place to call their own, but there is always a condition (verses 16 and 17) that they keep faithful to God.

Does God set the boundaries of modern nation states? This has been a dilemma for the peoples of the Middle East, for modern Israel has claimed the divine gift of its ancient lands despite their occupation by Arabs for over a thousand years. What would we say about our own national land? Is it something to be bartered or sold? Does it belong to the whole nation or to a few landowners?

In verses 8, 10 and 11, the word used is that they will 'occupy' the land, not that they will own it. We may see this as a sign that we are all tenants in God's earth, given the use of it, stewards who are responsible to God.

✷ *Fruitfulness of the land*
  and faithfulness of the people went hand in hand.
  Lord, may we know both of these blessings.

Day 98   *John 15.12-17*

Friends of Christ

Jesus chose them; that is how it happened. He met Philip and said, 'Follow me.' He saw a man named Matthew and said, 'Follow me.' 'He appointed twelve to be his companions' (Mark 3.14). This is something like the call of God to Abraham and Moses to be pioneers of the way. But now they are called 'friends'. So on that last evening at the table, Jesus reminds them that he has called them and will not desert them, for they are bound closely as the branch of the vine (verse 5).

Just as the old covenant at Sinai required a standard of conduct of the Israelites, so their new binding together carries with it a law. It is a commandment, not an imperative, not to be argued. But how can love be a law? Isn't love an emotion?

We have to recognize that the word used in the New Testament means a settled direction of the heart and mind to respect and care for others, even at great personal cost. God loves us like that. So that is the characteristic of his people.

✷ *Jesu, Jesu,*
  fill us with your love,
  show us how to serve
the neighbours we have from you.

T S Colvin, Ghana (© Agape, USA)

Day 99   1 John 3.11-18
Community life

A 'father in God' addresses his children. This is the style of the letter (2.1; 2.12; 2.18; 2.28 and so on). In simple direct language, he calls them to reveal the way in which the family of God should live together. We are to love our fellow Christians (verse 14) and this involves a practical compassion (verse 17).

This teaching is not obscure but is disobeyed in many aspects of the life of the Church. There are divisions between rich and poor. In one parish, district, circuit, or diocese, there may be a wealthy congregation and a poor one side by side and very little is done to even things up. In the world, there are rich churches, with great resources of land and investments, and very poor churches which struggle to find a hut in which to worship. Little has been done to change this.

Love in the family is also denied when nationalism and old animosity persists. How does God view the relations between Orthodox and Catholics in Eastern Europe, between mainline Churches and Base Christian Communities in Latin America, between Catholics and Protestants in Northern Ireland?

✷ *Have patience with us, Lord,*
  and teach us every day how to be your true family.

For personal reflection or group discussion

- Can we properly apply the theme of God's chosen people to our own nation and its history?
- If we think of the Church as the New Israel, what are the qualities of this people – not in theory but in our own experience?

Day 100   *Galatians 3.23 to 4.7*

Children of God

Paul knew that the Galatian Christians were being pressed by other teachers to accept the whole body of Jewish Law. He wrote to strengthen them, to recognize the freedom which was the gift of God in the work of Christ.

In these verses, the main thoughts are:

- the Law was essential but is no longer our authority;
- our new position through faith is that of children in God's household with all the rights of children;
- some of us were slaves but now we have been set free by one who became a servant for us;
- the sign of our freedom is that we know God as our true father.

Meditate on verse 28. The family of God is not divided by the divisions of the world. There are no categories which define our status. We are not listed by God as black or white, learned or simple, clergy or laity. Our denominational labels have little meaning here. There is a new creation in Christ; the twelve tribes of the old covenant become one body of Christ in the new.

* *One holy Church of God appears*
    Through every age and race,
 Unwasted by the lapse of years,
    Unchanged by changing place.

 Her priests are all God's faithful sons,
    To serve the world raised up;
 The pure in heart her baptized ones,
    Love, her communion cup.

Samuel Longfellow 1819-92

Day 101   *2 Corinthians 5.11-19*

The mission of God

It was the great gift of Paul to see that the gospel of Jesus was universal. It would have been quite possible for the followers of Jesus to have remained as an offshoot, a heresy of Judaism, restricted to a local group in Palestine. In his travelling ministry and in his thinking, Paul showed that such a limitation would be unfaithful to Jesus. Christ died for all (verse 14) and so the gift of new life is offered to all (verse 17). This new life is a second creation story; the new world is being made by God and, just as in Genesis, the Spirit now moves the human heart to hear, receive and be renewed by the gospel.

The group of those who believe is given a great commission: the ministry of reconciliation. The human family has strayed from the purpose of God. Paul was very conscious of the dark side of human life (e.g. Romans 1.18-32) and saw in Christ God's act to rescue and remake the world. This is reconciliation; men and women will be at one with God. Here is the calling to our local congregation: to share in the mission of God.

✶ *You have made us new in Christ*
and called us to be servants of the gospel.
Holy Spirit, guide our lives, unite our fellowship,
give us courage and let Christ rule our hearts.

Day 102   *Matthew 5.43-48*

Breaking the cycle

In 1 John 3.11-18, we were challenged to live the love of God within the Christian community. Here in Matthew, Jesus calls us to go much further and so break the cycle of revenge.

Human history has been disfigured by feuds which continue for generations. To justify some cruelty today, the story is told of what cruelty we received ages ago. So Romanians may speak of Hungarians, Serbs of Croats, Arabs of Christians and so on and on.

The cycle of violence has to be broken by one party refusing to play the revenge game; only then will a new peace for humanity be secured. Jesus goes far beyond our old tribalism and our legalism to love for our enemies. The old Law could justify violence (verse 38). In his book *The Cost of Discipleship* Dietrich Bonhoeffer argues that in Christ 'wars of faith' are impossible: 'The only way to overcome our enemy is by loving him.' And, in his death, Dietrich Bonhoeffer showed what it meant to love those who executed him.

At the end of a terrible civil war, Abraham Lincoln said, 'With malice toward none; with charity for all; with firmness in the right, as God gives us to see the right, let us strive on to finish the work we are in; to bind up the nation's wounds, to care for him who shall have borne the battle, and for his widow and orphan' *(Speech at the Second Inaugural, March 4, 1865)*. May the world know that voice.

✳ *We pray for the victims of war and those who profit by war – the nations who produce and sell ever more sophisticated weapons; we pray for those who use them to fight and kill. Forgive them for their trade in human blood . . . Make them and us more aware of your image in each human being.*
   Prayer from Mozambique, from Oceans of Prayer (NCEC)

Day 103   Luke 7.1-10
Beyond Israel

It was not a novel event for healing to be given outside the Israelite community. The story of Elisha and Naaman (2 Kings 5) is a great example of faith rewarded. But here in Luke's Gospel, the healing stands as a sign of faith, faith which was unexpected, when those around Jesus showed little confidence in him. For a Roman centurion to have faith in Jesus must have been like a senior colonial officer going for help to a practitioner of native medicine. It was surprising faith, humble faith.

So the community of those who recognized in Jesus the authority of God was not to be confined to one nation. In the old covenant, the line had been drawn around those twelve tribes of Israel. At times any blurring of the line was seen to be sinful, as we read in Ezra 9 where mixed marriages were disclosed. Yet there was also hope for a much wider salvation, as in Isaiah 49.6, and it was that dimension which this Roman soldier confirmed.

We may not narrow down the grace of Christ. When his healing reaches beyond our tradition, our community, our style of theology, then we praise him for his grace.

✳ *Come Holy God,*
   Come, loving Source of our life,
   Come, healing Light.
   Come healing Light,

Source of our life,
Come, healing Light.
India,
from Oceans of Prayer (NCEC)

Day 104 *Daniel 6.10-23*

The security of faith

Because the people of Israel were caught between great empires, they lived with risk. They had no great wall or mountain range to protect them. Often they needed encouragement to remain faithful to their calling and not to slip into the ways of great powers which threatened them. The book of Daniel is written as a call to trust in God; that is where true security is to be found. These verses present the greatest possible risk – a horrible death and no resting place for the body – but the Lord is there to rescue his servant.

In the time of Jesus, the imperial power was that of Rome and it could become a danger to Jewish life and faith. 'Do not fear those who kill the body, but cannot kill the soul,' said Jesus (Matthew 10.28). Faith is the ultimate security. This is not easy for us to believe in a world where insurance and security are about our homes, possessions and pensions. But it is still true; the people of God only survive through faith. Wealth is no security for the Church (Revelation 3.17), nor is political power, but faith survives in the lion-pit of persecution.

✳ **O God**
Our suffering sigh in heaven is heard
and faith in you will ease all pain.
We shall not give up! *Gershon Anderson, Sierra Leone*
from Oceans of Prayer (NCEC)

Day 105 *Hebrews 11.32-40; 2 Thessalonians 3.1-5*

The crown of faith

Time is too short for me to tell the stories of Dietrich Bonhoeffer, Oscar Romero, Janani Luwum, of Terry Waite and his companions in captivity. Through faith, they resisted great powers, stood for justice and trusted God's promises. In China during the cultural revolution, they were tortured and hunted, crushed under Communism, bodies and minds battered each day, men and women of whom the world is not worthy. They were refugees in Lebanon, Sudan and Angola, hiding in caves and holes in the ground. Others by faith used medical skills to open blind eyes, to restore dying babies to their mothers' arms and overcome dangerous diseases. Others again reached out to the lost and forgotten in great cities, bringing food and respect to the homeless and peace to the dying. (*Write your own version of these verses, remembering all the faithful people who have been your inspiration*). All these won God's accolade for their faith.

Therefore, as we are surrounded by this great host of faithful people, we throw off every hindrance and run the same race of faith, looking to Jesus.

✷ *Teach us, Lord Jesus, to find in you the life to be lived, the joy to be shared, the bread to be eaten, the truth to be told*
and the peace to be given; for your name's sake.
Mother Teresa, words adapted for use in the
Methodist Prayer Handbook 1993/4

Day 106   *Psalm 98*

Songs of joy

There is much that is solemn and even grim in the Bible and in Christian tradition. We cannot evade that. All our preaching and prayer leads us to the cross, the point where the abiding love of God met the blindness and cruelty of the human family. But there is also a symphony of celebration. There are shouts of joy which fill this psalm.

The message is that God who created us and called us his people is not defeated, demolished, dead. Those who deny God, whatever their philosophy, also live in God's world, surrounded by God's creative power. Every life which is lived in respect and courage and truth is a victory to sing about. Where an old enmity is overcome and new trust is given, there this psalm applies.

For we see in the resurrection the assurance of God's victory. God's people are not left alone like the stragglers of a defeated army. The Lord is ahead of us, for even the grave could not hold him. After reading the psalm, look at Philippians 2.9-11.

✷ *Lord our God, we pray for those who are defeated*
by pain, sorrow, despair or loneliness.
May they know the victory of love,
the song of hope and a glimpse of glory.

For personal reflection or group discussion

- Sometimes churches have created barriers between people as well as breaking barriers down. Which is more true of the churches in your area?
- Jesus did not promise that his followers would escape physical danger and pain, but this is often what we expect and pray for. Should we pray like that?

ACTION

List all the people who have helped you to enter into Christian faith. See how many different traditions and countries are represented. Express thanks for them, by writing a prayer or saying a word to those close to you.

REMINDER: *Have you sent off your order form on page 120?*

PRAY FOR THE PEACE OF JERUSALEM

Notes based on the New Revised Standard Version by

Harry Hagopian

Harry Hagopian is an Armenian Christian from Jerusalem. For many years he was Assistant General Secretary of the Middle East Council of Churches (MECC) – an ecumenical organization which represents the region's 14 million local Christians. He has been particularly involved in the Council's humanitarian work with refugees, human rights advocacy, interpretation and the communication ministry. In 1996, he was appointed Director of the MECC in Jerusalem.

Jerusalem out-ranks all other cities of the Bible in prominence and wealth of sacred associations. It appears in nearly two-thirds of the books of the Old Testament and in nearly half of the books of the New Testament.

1996 is destined to be a special year for Jerusalem. It has been earmarked for political discussions by Palestinians and Israelis over the future status of the Holy City – following the PLO-Israel Declaration of Principles in September 1993.

All three monotheistic faiths have an historic claim to the city. For Jews, Jerusalem is home to their holiest site, the Western Wall, the only remaining Wall of the Second Temple. For Christians, it is the place of Christ's crucifixion and resurrection, and birthplace of Christianity. For Muslims, it is the third holiest city of Islam whence the prophet Mohammed ascended into heaven.

Religious passions are matched by political ones. The Israeli government is determined to keep Jerusalem its 'united and eternal capital'. To that end, the city is now ringed with densely populated Jewish settlements, and the traditional Arab majority in East Jerusalem has recently been reversed. The Palestinian National Authority insists that East Jerusalem will be the capital of a new Palestine. Now, more than ever before, prayers for the peace of Jerusalem are needed. If there can be religious and political co-existence in this 'faithful city' as Zechariah calls it (8.3), there can surely be peace in the Middle East.

Recommended Reading
Whose Promised Land? Colin Chapman (Lion Publishing)
Jerusalem, A Shared Trust? (MECC July 1990, issue #8)

Day 107
1 Chronicles 11.1-8 and 17.1-15

Jerusalem and the desire for a temple

We find an account here of the building of the famous city walls that greet every visitor to the Old City. The walls remain intact, but both Temples built in Jerusalem were destroyed by the Romans in AD70 and AD135 respectively. All that remains of the second Temple is the Western Wall, where Jews gather every day to pray. Nowadays, there is even a service that accepts prayer requests by fax and then places them in the cracks of the ancient wall!

Built on the site of the ancient Jewish Temple, at right angles to the Western Wall, is Al Aqsa Mosque and the Dome of the Rock. Its recently restored golden dome dominates the Jerusalem skyline and is a constant reminder of the presence of Islam in the Holy City. However, some religious Jews, called the Temple Mount Faithful, want to destroy the Muslim complex and build the third temple.

The issue of the Temple today should not be one of confrontation. Surely, a religious site holy to Muslims in an area also holy to Jews, should be a sign of how both faiths, related by their common father Abraham, are intertwined in this city. And just a few minutes' walk away is the Church of the Holy Sepulchre, a Christian holy place where tradition says Christ was crucified. Shouldn't the peaceful sharing of such Holy Land then be symbolic of the mutual tolerance and respect that needs to infuse current political dialogue and underpin any real political progress toward peace?

✷ *Pray that all those who have played a part in making Jerusalem into a theatre of division and conflict turn afresh to God, the God of Abraham and Isaac, the God of Mohammed and the God and Father of our Lord Jesus Christ. Pray for the increased sensitivity of Jewish, Christian and Muslim leaders in Jerusalem towards each other and their different traditions and beliefs.*

Day 108   *Psalm 68.1-16 and 28-35*

Belief that God is present there

This psalm expresses the belief that God, whose majesty stretches over Israel, is not only present there, but is all powerful, awesome – and in control. Some Palestinian Christians have been wrestling with such verses which refer to God as the 'God of Israel'. Surely, God is also the God of Palestinian Christians? Are we to believe, they ask, that this God of Israel is now causing Palestinians to be dispersed? How does God allow Christians to face persecution, torture and hardship, to be treated as second class citizens in the land of Jesus – and be forced to forsake their ancestral property for foreign climes? N.B. Today it would take only four jumbo jets to remove all Christians from Jerusalem.

An ecumenical Palestinian Liberation Theology Group was recently formed at St George's Anglican Cathedral in Jerusalem to biblically explore and pray about these issues. Its members say their faith in a God who loves all those created in his image – whether Jewish, Christian or Muslim – has been restored. After all, they too are God's children and God's people. Colin Chapman, author of *Whose Promised Land?* goes further. He quotes Paul in one of his earliest letters, describing all followers of Jesus, both Jews and Gentiles, as 'Abraham's seed' and therefore inheritors of the promise given to Abraham (Galatians 3.26-29; Ephesians 2.14-20 and 3.6).

So, Palestinian Christians can also put their trust in the Lord of verse 5 as 'the father of orphans and protector of widows' who will give 'the desolate a home to live in' and who will lead out the prisoners to prosperity and provide for the needy. Palestinian refugees, prisoners and those who are oppressed can truly sing praises to God's name (verse 4). God is non-exclusive and non-tribal.

But with that must come belief in the sanctuary of God in his Holy City. Is our behaviour today in Jerusalem – whether Palestinian or Jew – fit for the presence of God?

✶ *Pray for the Liberation Theology Group at St George's Cathedral as it attempts to discover an all-inclusive understanding of our selective attitudes as 'Children of God', as well as for a renewed sense of awe in the presence of God in Jerusalem today.*

Day 109 *Isaiah 25.6-9*

A vision of God's banquet for all the nations

This is the Palestinian Liberation Theology Group's inclusive God at work – describing the feast he will prepare for all peoples and assuring us of the Salvation he will bring.

It is the day anticipated by many who have suffered in Jerusalem, who have seen political processes falter or fail, promises broken, and self-interest rule.

'Then the Lord God will wipe away the tears from all faces' (verse 8). It is surely this vision of the future that must keep bigotry, intolerance and hatred at bay. It does not, however, mean Christians can abdicate responsibility for the present. Human rights' workers, staff of non-governmental organizations, church workers organizing rehabilitation for the suffering, and encounter groups between those of different faiths, must all continue in their uphill struggle for peace in Jerusalem. They too, in the midst of their busy and at times frustrating lives, must not lose sight of the day of salvation.

✸ *Pray for the Israelis and Palestinians who are weary and exhausted through their peacemaking efforts.*

Day 110 *Isaiah 60.1-7 and 15-22*

Written after the Babylonian exile, believing that Jerusalem will become an international Centre

Many Jews dream of their people coming to Jerusalem from all the nations of the world – an in-gathering after centuries of exile. Indeed, thousands of Jews do arrive in Israel each month to settle. They are guaranteed citizenship.

But if the people of God are not only Jews, but all followers of Christ who seek righteousness and peace, what a magnet their presence would be to the city of Jerusalem! This city would indeed become transformed into a shining symbol of peace. However, the prospect of an end to violence and destruction, the prospect of 'calling the walls of Jerusalem Salvation and its gates Praise' is one that still seems far off.

In recent years, the walls of Jerusalem have witnessed frequent bloody clashes between Palestinian stone-throwers and the Israeli army, with tear gas and gunfire spewing from its gates. Chilling fear often stalks the old city's narrow winding streets and colourful souks: Israeli settlers, Palestinian militants and tourists rub shoulders, one wary of the other. Violence is never far from the surface: in minutes it can transform a bustling scene. Shutters are pulled down on the Arab shop fronts in the old city whose windows display Bethlehem olive wood carvings of the Holy Family, Armenian pottery, mother-of-pearl and hand-woven rugs.

The vision for Jerusalem here in Isaiah is the peacemakers' dream. But such peace comes with the statement that the people shall all be righteous. What does that say to us today about where the quest for peace should start?

✱ *Pray for the righteousness of church leaders, politicians and individuals in many countries as they discuss the future of Jerusalem.*

Day 111   Isaiah 65.17-25

Vision of peace – and the innocent

Many Palestinian Christians today draw comfort from this passage. After the creation of the state of Israel in 1948, between 60 and 70 per cent of Palestinian Christians fled or were driven out of their ancestral homes. My own family home still stands in West Jerusalem: it was occupied by a Jewish family hours after my family, dispossessed, fled in the mistaken belief they would soon return home. Over the years, many other families have seen their land, with the crops and the vineyards their families tended for centuries, taken from them by force and now worked by others.

One of the greatest tragedies of the last half century of conflict is how women – of all faiths – have 'borne children for calamity'. Palestinian mothers see their sons gaoled, beaten, maimed or killed; Jewish mothers see their sons hated and reviled, injured or brutalized as they carry out their compulsory military service patrolling the unwelcoming streets of Jerusalem and the West Bank.

A group of Jewish women, called 'Women in Black', held a vigil every Friday in downtown Jerusalem calling for an end to Israeli military occupation. Their dress changed to white when the PLO-Israel Declaration was signed, in the hope that this was indeed the beginning of a peace where their sons and daughters would no longer face death, where 'no more shall there be an infant that lives but for a few days, or an old person who does not live out a lifetime.'

Equally, a crucial principle of forging true peace is spelt out here in verse 17: 'The former things shall not be remembered or come to mind.' How often have peace proposals been scuppered because one side hurls accusations of past atrocities at the other? How often have politicians whipped up opposition to peace by reminding their people what the enemy has done and how it cannot be trusted in the future? True forgiveness is painful and often unpopular – working to wipe out the past in order to move to a time when 'no more shall the sound of weeping be heard' in Jerusalem' (verse 19).

* *Pray for a sense of true forgiveness among all sides involved in the Palestinian-Israeli conflict and for those organizations working today to promote subsequent reconciliation.*

Day 112   Luke 19.41-44 and 23.27-31
Jesus' tears over the future of his people

Jesus' words seem as relevant today as in Biblical times. As opportunities for peace in Jerusalem have come and gone in recent times, it appears that 'the things that make for peace' are hidden from peoples' eyes (verse 42).

The consequences of missing the opportunity for peace are equally relevant. As in yesterday's passage, here is a prediction that mothers will say 'Blessed are the barren, and the wombs that never bore, and the breasts that never nursed.' Given the importance placed on having children in the Middle East (remember Sarah's plight of barrenness or Elizabeth's joy at being pregnant after so long), it is a prediction that strikes at the very fabric of oriental society. The family is the collective unit around which that society operates, unlike the individualism often cherished in the West. A woman's identity is still largely centred around her children. Great joy comes from their birth and great pain from the inability to conceive, emotions shared by Palestinians and Jews alike. In addition, for Jews, the emphasis placed on having children comes in the wake of the brutal death of six million Jews in the Holocaust. Today, in an attempt to replace those killed, it is said that Israel has the highest rate of *in vitro* fertilization (IVF) in the world. It is a powerful image therefore for mothers to see the childless as blessed.

Jesus' weeping over the city of Jerusalem was not a one-off occasion. There has been little cause for him to cease weeping as people have continued to reject him and his teachings and failed to see him as the Prince of peace.

* *Pray for the acceptance of Jesus as prime peacemaker in the Holy City.*

Day 113   Psalm 122
Pray for the peace of Jerusalem

This is an appeal to all nations to pray for the peace of the Holy City. David wishes prosperity to those who work and pray for its peace – a peace 'for the sake of relatives and friends' who live there (verse 8). But to what end should people seek the good of Jerusalem? 'For the sake of the house of the LORD our God', says David (verse 9).

Peace is often concluded for pragmatic, political self-interest, or because of the strategic importance and the resources a country can offer. In its history, Jerusalem has often been a pawn between nations, kings and governments. Today Jerusalem is still being fought over. Since 1993, political controversy has raged around whose capital it should be: Palestinians claiming East Jerusalem as theirs; Jews claiming the whole city as theirs!

Claims over religious ownership or guardianship of the holy sites are equally contentious. Muslims hold the key to the Church of the Holy Sepulchre because Christians have often bitterly disagreed how it should be denominationally divided and managed. Even who should clean a windowsill or sweep the floor has been under dispute! Jordan wants to retain custodianship of the Dome of the Rock complex, while the Palestinian National Authority claim it as their duty. Even Saudi Arabia wants to enter the fray!

Few people work for the good of Jerusalem as a symbol of the healing power – the reconciliation and forgiveness – of the Lord our God; a place where all God's people can come in peace to 'give thanks to the name of the Lord'.

Christians have a duty to pray for the peace of the earthly city of Jerusalem – remembering at the same time that the true worship of God can never again be localized either there or at any other place on earth (John 4.21). The new Jerusalem of Revelation is no earthly city but one that will come down 'out of heaven from God' (21.10).

* *Pray for the peace of Jerusalem.*

For personal reflection or group discussion

What do you know about 'the Forgotten Faithful' – the indigenous Christians of the Holy Land who have been witnessing to their faith since the Church of the Pentecost?

Do you tend to forget their stake in Jerusalem and see the conflict in terms of a stark Muslim/Jewish confrontation?

Does striving towards mutual respect and accommodation of all three faiths, as much as different denominations, have anything to say to your own situation at home? Does it question any intolerance or prejudice you may harbour?

ACTION

- When visiting the Holy Land, make sure you meet with some of its 'living stones' – local Christians – as well as visiting sites of historic and religious importance.

- Consider inviting someone from a church in the Holy Land to speak to your group/congregation, or develop a prayer link between a local church/group and your own.

- Perhaps your church can 'twin' with a church in the Holy City – providing Arab Christians much-needed spiritual comfort and moral support.

- In conversations with friends and acquaintances, do not shy away from taking a stand that might be politically unpopular: Jesus himself never courted popularity and acceptance, but spoke out strongly against the injustices and oppression of the establishment.

PROCESSES

Learn to love, help to heal.

Remember not to judge a light by the size of its container. Even a small oil lamp can give light to a big room.

USEFUL ADDRESSES

Middle East Council of Churches
P O Box 1248
Jerusalem

Christian Aid
PO Box 100
London SE1 7RL

PEACE WITH JUSTICE

Notes based on text from the Jewish Publication Society by

Albert H Friedlander

Rabbi Albert Friedlander, Dean of the Leo Baeck College, trains Reform rabbis, and is minister of the Westminster Synagogue in London. He is President of the World Conference of Religions for Peace (UK), and has edited many of the annual Week of Prayer for World Peace prayer leaflets. Theologian, historian and writer of over a dozen books, he is active in interfaith work, and was the Jewish advisor to Franco Zeffirelli's film 'Jesus of Nazareth'.

The prophecies and teachings speak out of dark times when evil ruled and when humanity yearned for the coming of God's Kingdom on earth. But when has that not been the case? After a century of genocide and human suffering, humanity yearns for a time of peace and knows that peace can only come when justice prevails. That is a task in daily life for men and women who are concerned to fight against lies and exploitation, and who seek the vision of a world without war.

Day 114 *Psalm 140*

A matter of words

This is an angry Psalm, where the desire for peace in the world is blended with awareness that peace cannot come into existence without justice being done. The Psalmist recognizes that the world is filled with violent evil-doers, and that it is in the nature of evil to stir up war: in the time of violence, evil will flourish.

'They have sharpened their tongue like a serpent;
vipers venom is under their lips' (verse 3)

is a reminder that words are weapons which can hurt or destroy. The psalmist often compares evil tongues to arrows and swords, or speaks of them as poisonous. 'Their venom is like the venom of a serpent' (Psalm 58.4). Our own words are not always an antidote against evil, but our prayers for peace at this time at least present an alternative vision to a world sick of war. Perhaps that is why the religious vision is attacked by those who prefer evil, who try to stifle and ensnare the voice of faith.

At that point, we turn to God 'the strength of our salvation', the opponent of evil, who gives us assurance that justice will prevail, that the 'upright will dwell in God's presence'.

✸ *After the night, we pray for dawn.*
After war, we pray for peace.
O Lord, fill our hearts with compassion and love,
so that we may walk through the darkness
and emerge into a morning filled with Divine Love.

Day 115   Deuteronomy 28.58-68

The bread of life

Starvation had brought the children of Israel to Egypt; there they became slaves. Moses brought them out of that land, and they entered into a covenant with God. They were warned that the breaking of that covenant would have severe consequences (verses 58-59). Sickness, starvation, and plagues ravage a land where the teachings of the Bible are forgotten. The world hungers for bread – the bread of heaven as well as harvests of the land. The children of Israel here represent all humanity, and those who reject God's commandments to love their neighbour and to share the bounties of the world. In an immoral society, humans serve other gods 'which thou hast not known, even wood and stone' (verse 64). Everyone who is estranged from God and the teachings of justice is as a refugee, wandering lonely 'with a trembling heart, and failing eyes, and in languishing of soul . . . in doubt and fear' (verses 65-66). But we can reject the darkness of Egypt and turn to the light of God.

✸ *We praise you, O God, Who givest food to all.*
In lands of hunger, feed the starving;
and in lands where evil rules,
may the Bread of Heaven, the words of the Bible,
sustain those who hunger for the Divine Word.

Day 116   Isaiah 2.2-5

Vision of peace

The Bible is not only a book reflecting the problems and hopes of the past; it speaks for the present, and for the future. Every generation looks forward to the time when all nations and people will be united in worshipping the One God, when all will turn in love towards one another. And yet, throughout human history, we have killed one another in cruel wars. The God of justice does not want warfare; and Isaiah reminds us that God's word will come to judge and to instruct at the end of days:

'And he shall judge between the nations . . .
And they shall beat their swords into plowshares . . .
Nations shall not lift up swords against nations,
Neither shall they learn war any more' (Isaiah 2.4).

A few years ago, in the old East German Republic, I visited churches in East Berlin and in Leipzig and met with Christian pacifists. A number of them wore the symbol of a sword beaten into a plowshare. One told me that his daughter had worn the symbol in her school. But she was summoned to the office and told that this disqualified her from her university place: she was an enemy of the state! But the symbol endures for our time – nations must *not* learn war any more, so that the world can come to the top of God's mountains and meet in peace.

✷ *O Lord our God: we pray that all implements of war may be turned into tools for peace.*
May the vision of the Eternal Kingdom,
where the lion and the lamb lie down together,
become tomorrow's reality in our world.

Day 117 *Jeremiah 7.1-15*
The only way

'Every sanctuary sends out its messengers saying:
The temple of the LORD, the temple of the LORD, the temple of the LORD are these' (Jeremiah 7.4).

But can these messengers be trusted? The words we want to hear – the message out of the sacred texts – are their own validation, established by the impact they have upon the world. If people do not live by the word, texts become a disguise for acts of violence and war. The prophet stands in front of the Temple, warning the people about to enter its gates that priests and people enter a world of lies if their actions have not already given proof that the vision of justice and peace is practised in their homes and in their lands. God will only reward them if

'ye thoroughly amend your ways and your doings. If ye thoroughly execute justice between a man and his neighbour; if ye oppress not the stranger, the fatherless, and the widow, and shed not innocent blood in this place, neither walk after other gods to your hurt . . .' (Jeremiah 7.5-6).

Jeremiah was an 'outsider', respected for his priestly background, his visions and undoubted genuineness – but hated because he taught peace in a time of war. His books were burned, he was hunted, attacked, and thrown into prison. He still taught that peace and justice, intertwined, were the only way into the sanctuary of God – and to God.

✷ *Lord our God, lead us back into the sanctuaries*
  where the Bible is read, and where people listen.
  Make our homes temples of worship, and let us live
  as brothers and sisters who seek truth and compassion.

Day 118   Isaiah 42.1-4

The challenge of suffering

Waiting for the messianic age concentrates our minds upon those who suffer: we recognize the divine in every tortured human being. A rabbinical text tells of a student who went to his rabbi and asked, 'When will the Messiah come?'

'Go to the gates of Rome and look among the beggars. You will find him there. Ask him,' was the reply.

He went to one of the gates, and found the Messiah! 'When will you come?' he asked with fear and trembling.

'Today!' said the Messiah.

That evening, the student reported sadly to his teacher: 'He said "today!" – and he didn't come!'

'You misunderstood him,' replied the rabbi. '"Today " means "IF you want me to come today. If you live your lives that way, then I will surely come today".'

Our hopes for a Messianic Time – or for a Second Coming – depend upon our response to this text which sees the divine message conveyed by human suffering. A brilliant populist politician has less to say to us than the hungering and dispossessed who pass us silently in the street:

'He shall not cry, or lift up
Nor cause his voice to be heard in the street.
A bruised reed shall he not break
And the dimly burning wick shall he not quench' (verses 2-3).

But that person's suffering proclaims the presence of God among those who suffer in the world, and opens our eyes to the messianic vision of a just, peaceful world.

✱ *O God of Love and Compassion:*
teach us to understand suffering.
May we be kind to those who are in pain;
and may our own pain lead us to greater understanding,
so that we too may accept the compassion of others.

Day 119   Zechariah 9.9-10
The way of the meek

Much of our study of the Bible remains incomplete if we ignore the poetic language through which the great teachings are expressed. Parallelism, for example, where the second line repeats the thought of the first line, is very much part of yesterday's Isaiah passage. Here too, this pattern prevails:

'Rejoice greatly, O daughter of Zion,
Shout, O daughter of Jerusalem;
Behold, thy king cometh unto thee,
He is triumphant and victorious,
Lowly, and riding upon an ass,
Even upon a colt the foal of an ass' (Zechariah 9.9).

The first two lines are really identical; but the second part brings its problems. Can a king at the same time be 'victorious, triumphant' and also 'lowly, riding upon an ass'? The anointed King of Israel is seen as a triumphant hero. Anointing was part of the ritual of enthronement; the Hebrew word, '*moshiach*', 'messiah' means literally 'the anointed one'. At the same time, he is identified with the humble and meek. The mighty stallion of the victorious general is replaced by the humble donkey. Perhaps it is not a king who enters here, but a humble, lowly pilgrim – and that is a path we can follow. Who is humble? The person who conquers his or her spirit – and who thus becomes 'mighty' is an old teaching. It is a pathway leading towards God's Kingdom.

✱ *O God, if there is a special kingdom for the meek,*
let it be in our midst.

Day 120   Genesis 6.5-8
The power of goodness

Every once in a while we despair when we look at the world. The world is filled with evil, and human beings destroy each other. There is war instead of peace, injustice in the place of justice, and we see humans whose 'every imagination of the thoughts of his heart was only evil continually' (Genesis 5.5).

We despair; and it seems to us that God must despair as well. But at this point we discover that God can discern a good person where we have already lost hope.

'Noah found grace in the eyes of the LORD' (Genesis 6.8), we are told. The world and humanity is saved through that person. Why? In the next sentence, the Bible gives us an answer:

'Noah was in his generation a man righteous and whole-hearted; Noah walked with God' (Genesis 6.9).

Tradition considers every word of the Bible to be essential. What does 'in his generation' add? Some of our teachers said: 'In that evil generation even a flawed human being, Noah, could be considered righteous – in another time and place he would not have been acceptable.' But the majority decided: if one can be good in an evil time, one must be very righteous. And that was tradition's judgment on Noah. When we think of righteous Christians who hid and saved Jews in the time of the Holocaust, we understand our text: one person, in an evil time, can save the world. Tradition teaches: to save one human life means saving a whole world!

✳ *O Lord, who is righteous? Clear thou me from hidden faults.*
Let me not exalt myself above others, but let me learn that humanity walks together through the storm,
that we are redeemed by good deeds and by Your grace.

For personal reflection, group discussion and ACTION

Make a list of ways to become involved in mediation and peace-making. Underline those which challenge you to become involved. Pray the Universal Prayer for Peace:

> *Lead me from Death to Life*
> *from Falsehood to Truth*
> *Lead me from Despair to Hope*
> *from Fear to Trust*
> *Lead me from Hate to Love*
> *from War to Peace*
> *Let Peace fill our Heart*
> *our World, our Universe*
> *Peace – Peace – Peace*

IBRA International Appeal

Where does your money go?

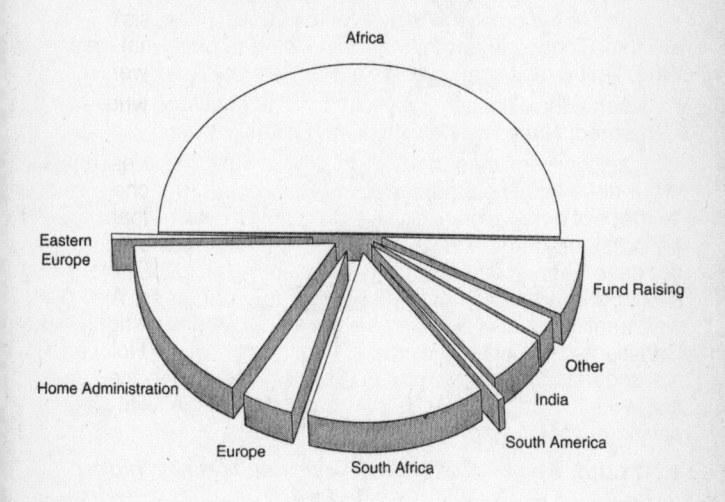

Pie chart with segments labelled: Africa, Eastern Europe, Fund Raising, Home Administration, Other, India, Europe, South Africa, South America

IBRA also supports work in many other countries where some Christians are not able to pay for their Bible Reading notes.

We need to respond to requests from former Eastern Europe, Romania and Estonia particularly and provide extra help for the Gilbert Isles.

SO PLEASE HELP US AGAIN BY GIVING GENEROUSLY

Place your gift in the envelope provided and give it to your IBRA representative,

or send it direct to
The IBRA International Appeal,
1020 Bristol Road, Selly Oak,
Birmingham B29 6LB, Great Britain

THANK YOU FOR YOUR HELP

A Collection Of Collections

LITURGY OF LIFE

Compiled by Donald Hilton.
In corporate acts of worship in all the mainstream churches the same basic elements can be seen. This anthology broadly follows the liturgy of the Churches bringing into the sanctuary the everyday experiences and thoughts which interlock with the main components of Christian worship.

Liturgy of Life is intended both to aid personal devotion and reflection, and also to provide material for Christian education and worship.

FLOWING STREAMS

Compiled by Donald Hilton.
Countless streams of human experiences flow through the Bible narratives and the same emotions flow through human life in our time. In this anthology these contemporary experiences mingle, page by page, with the experiences recorded in the Bible. Everyday life thus becomes a comment on the Bible stories, and the biblical events help to interpret our life today.

TURN BUT A STONE

By Edmund Banyard
This new collection of prayers and meditations written by Edmund Banyard is intended as a stimulation to thought, both for personal devotion and as an aid in corporate worship. It expands on the themes of the Bible readings suggested in the *Joint Liturgical Group Lectionary* (JLG2).
Edmund's earlier book *Word Alive*, an anthology of works from around the world, was used as a companion to the previous lectionary (JLG1).

REFLECTIONS

By Cyril Franks.
The Gospels speak to us today and every day. In this collection of thirty-one readings from St Matthew's Gospel we are invited to draw nearer to Christ as we reflect on Matthew's writings in our daily lives. Each passage is accompanied by a thought-provoking meditation.

A WEALTH OF WORSHIP AND LEARNING RESOURCES FROM NCEC

Available from your local Christian bookshop or, in case of difficulty, from IBRA direct.

IBRA   1020 Bristol Road, Selly Oak,
Birmingham B29 6LB, Great Britain

Living Prayers for Today

A new series of prayers for everyday use, compiled by Maureen Edwards.

These prayers for all occasions are 'user friendly' to individuals, groups and churches. The prayers reflect insights that are both refreshing and challenging to our own spiritual development. They articulate feelings and longings we often find hard to express.

IBRA

Available from your local Christian bookshop or, in case of difficulty from:

**IBRA, 1020 Bristol Road
Selly Oak,
Birmingham B29 6LB
Great Britain**

What next?

See the note on page 7 and then either order a copy of *Words for Today* or *Light for our Path* from your bookseller, or detach and complete the form below.

✂ ---

I would like to read the Bible regularly with IBRA. Please send information about your books of daily Bible reading notes.

Name _____

Address _____

_____

_____

_____ Postcode _____

Send this form to:

INTERNATIONAL BIBLE READING ASSOCIATION
1020 Bristol Road
Selly Oak
Birmingham
B29 6LB Great Britain